Complete Conditioning for
BASKETBALL

Greg Brittenham, MS Kinesiology
Strength and Conditioning Coach
New York Knicks

Human Kinetics

Library of Congress Cataloging-in-Publication Data

Brittenham, Greg.
    Complete conditioning for basketball / Greg Brittenham.
        p.   cm.
    ISBN 0-87322-881-2 (paper)
    1. Basketball--Training.   2. Physical education and training.
3. Physical fitness.   I. Title.
GV885.35.B75   1995
796.323'07--dc20   95-13033
                                                                          CIP

ISBN: 0-87322-881-2

Developmental Editor: Elaine Mustain; **Assistant Editors:** Karen Bojda, Erin Cler, Ed Giles, Kirby Mittelmeier, and Julie Ohnemus; **Copyeditor:** Keith Appler; **Proofreader:** Julia Anderson; **Typesetting and Layout:** Ruby Zimmerman; **Text Design:** Stuart Cartwright; **Photo Editor:** Boyd LaFoon; **Cover Design:** Jack Davis; **Photographer (cover and author):** George Kalinsky/Major League Graphics; **Photographers (interior):** John Sann and Jeff Soucek (p. xiii); **Printer:** United Graphics

Human Kinetics books are available at special discounts for bulk purchase. Special editions or book excerpts can also be created to specification. For details, contact the Special Sales Manager at Human Kinetics.

Printed in the United States of America   10   9   8   7

Human Kinetics
Web site: www.humankinetics.com

United States: Human Kinetics, P.O. Box 5076, Champaign, IL 61825-5076
800-747-4457
e-mail: humank@hkusa.com

Canada: Human Kinetics, 475 Devonshire Road, Unit 100, Windsor, ON N8Y 2L5
800-465-7301 (in Canada only)
e-mail: orders@hkcanada.com

Europe: Human Kinetics, Units C2/C3 Wira Business Park, West Park Ring Road
Leeds LS16 6EB, United Kingdom
+44 (0) 113 278 1708
e-mail: hk@hkeurope.com

Australia: Human Kinetics, 57A Price Avenue, Lower Mitcham, South Australia 5062
08 8277 1555
e-mail: liahka@senet.com.au

New Zealand: Human Kinetics, P.O. Box 105-231, Auckland Central
09-523-3462
e-mail: hkp@ihug.co.nz

For Mom

CONTENTS

FOREWORD

Early in my basketball career, my superior height was a tremendous advantage. As I moved on to higher levels of competition it became clear that height alone would not be enough to be a dominant player. So I spent many hours developing my basketball skills and, as a result, was fortunate to be on teams that won three state championships, an NCAA championship, and gold medals in the 1984 and 1992 Summer Olympic Games.

During my first few years as a pro, my skills carried me through. But I wasn't satisfied with the caliber of my play. My natural physical tools and basketball skills weren't enough to perform successfully night in and night out. I needed an *edge*. And I needed to be better able to handle the physical pounding of an 82-game regular season schedule. So when Greg Brittenham was hired by Pat Riley to be the strength and conditioning coach for the Knicks, I was ready to see what kind of training program he would prescribe.

Greg's approach to developing the *total athlete*—much of which is in *Complete Conditioning for Basketball*—is the best training program I've ever used. Since working with Greg, I have

- maintained my weight while decreasing my percent body fat significantly, meaning my overall physique is leaner and more muscular;
- increased my bench press training weight by nearly 45%, giving me much improved upper body strength;
- added 400 pounds to my inverted leg press, reflecting much greater lower body strength;
- raised my level of aerobic and anaerobic court conditioning to its highest mark ever; and
- developed far more agility and improved footwork.

And, for an added bonus, the workouts are challenging and include a variety of activities. Every day is different when you train Greg's way.

You won't be running boring wind sprints each practice. As the sample training sessions near the end of the book illustrate, Greg believes that workouts should include fun and variety to keep motivation high.

But what's best of all about the conditioning program Greg has developed is that it's highly functional—directly related to improving basketball performance; no wasted time and energy. My game has gone up another notch since using it. My movements on the court are quicker, stronger, and more skillful. I can also play more quality minutes instead of having to sit out and rest or being too tired to play at the same intensity in the fourth quarter as I did in the first.

The program is so valuable that, during the off-season, I have Greg fly down to Georgetown once a week to oversee my workouts. This insures that I am maximizing the benefits of my training. Maybe you can't have Greg pay you a weekly visit, but you can use the court drills and training suggestions in *Complete Conditioning for Basketball* to help you fully realize your physical potential. This may be the edge you need . . .

Patrick Ewing

PREFACE

During the '93-'94 season Hubert Davis, a back-up shooting guard for the Knicks, broke his hand and was sidelined for 7 weeks. Because the injury was so severe, Hubert was limited to lower body strength training and some light aerobic activity during the early stages of rehabilitation. His conditioning program consisted mostly of workouts on cardio equipment (i.e., stationary cycle, Stairmaster, Nordic Track, or treadmill) so he stayed in excellent aerobic shape, as indicated by the weekly submaximal tests we performed. In fact, he was in such good shape that he could run on the treadmill for an hour, nonstop, at an impressively fast pace.

After about 2 weeks, I took Hubert on to the basketball court for a little anaerobic sprint work. Just 5 minutes into the workout he was gasping for air. While Hubert was in great shape to endure the stress of a continual low-intensity activity such as running on a treadmill, he was in no shape to handle the high-intensity sprinting, cutting, and jumping necessary to play basketball effectively at the professional level. Although he could run at a moderate intensity for long stretches, he could not sustain the kind of shorter, all-out bursts of activity required to play basketball.

This example of subpar conditioning was the result of an injury. Unfortunately many healthy basketball players try to play the game without adequately preparing themselves for its physical demands. In other words, they lack **basketball conditioning**.

Complete Conditioning for Basketball is designed specifically for the development of the energy system used in basketball. The court drills outlined in this book are the same drills that Hubert Davis used to get back into "basketball shape"—actually surpassing his pre-injury conditioning level.

Here's another key point. Sport-specific skills in basketball include such fundamentals as dribbling, shooting, and passing. Other sports have their own set of skills, such as serving, spiking, digging, and setting in volleyball; and the serve, forehand, backhand, volley, and overhead shots in tennis; and so on. If two competing players possess equal sport-specific skills, it is the better *athlete* who will consistently come out on top. Why? Because the degree to which a player develops his or her athletic abilities—speed, power, endurance, coordination, agility—is what ultimately determines the level at which that player can perform sport-specific skills.

Unfortunately, many players fail to develop their athletic ability fully and instead focus only on improving their basketball skills. As a result, players typically become very good at performing basketball skills but lack the physical development to exploit those skills completely.

The purpose of this book is to lay the groundwork for coaches and athletes to look beyond the development of sport-specific skills as their primary mode of training. The text and illustrations provide an overview of the energy requirements for playing basketball effectively. Teaching physical fitness through the written word isn't easy. So, accompanying the text are more than 70 photographs of Doc Rivers demonstrating the exercises and activities, and 50 court drill diagrams that will help you develop your basketball-specific conditioning.

The diagrams are simple to follow, stress the appropriate energy system, and provide variety in daily routines. While the other components of athleticism (i.e., speed, strength, power, agility, coordination, etc.) will be enhanced as a by-product of the court drills, conditioning the specific energy system required to play competitive basketball is the main focus. Not only are the drills great for improving basketball conditioning, they're also a lot more fun than running the same wind sprints or "suicides" each practice. Plus, many of the drills include a skill component, so you can develop basketball skills and athleticism at the same time! Accompanying most of the diagrammed drills are some variations on the same pattern. So instead of having 50 drills to use, you have almost 150 drill options to choose from when designing a training routine.

In addition to detailing the principles and procedures of conditioning the energy system for basketball, I emphasize three essential components of athleticism. First, a warm-up and flexibility routine is critical to ensure that an athlete is ready to participate, whether playing a game or executing the drills in this book. Second, the primary focus of any training program should be the development of the trunk and low torso. To illustrate the importance of this region of the body, an entire chapter is devoted to training the "center of power." A powerful trunk and low torso will contribute to all aspects of basketball performance. Third, playing basketball requires several fundamental movement patterns (i.e., sprinting, shuffling, jumping, backward running, and movement combinations). So you'll find an entire section of the book designed to help you develop your movement skills. The court drills in chapters 8 and 9 will also incorporate a variety of movement, agility, and coordination skills that closely mimic those needed in a basketball game.

Complete Conditioning for Basketball is the next step in basketball training programs—the modern era of functional training where solid principles of conditioning combine with exercises and activities tailored to players' specific needs. There are no gimmicks or shortcuts to developing athleticism. But with hard work guided by the principles in this book, you and your team can reach top-level basketball condition.

ACKNOWLEDGMENTS

As an athletic performance specialist, I am indebted to all the teachers, coaches, and athletes who have greatly influenced my thinking. If it wasn't for their willingness to share concepts, drills, techniques, and ideas, I wouldn't have been able to write this book.

In the space provided here I can identify only a small number of the many people I would like to thank:

Coach Pat Riley and trainers Mike Saunders and Tim Walsh, who believed in the program and have allowed me the opportunity to work with the best athletes in the world, the New York Knicks.

Mark Grabow of the Golden State Warriors, Robin Pound of the Phoenix Suns, David Oliver of the Orlando Magic, and Rich Dalatri of the Cleveland Cavaliers, four respected colleagues in the NBA who put up with my questions and offered helpful answers.

Mark McKown, Director of Sports Development at the College of Charleston, who used the court drills for his fine basketball teams and provided feedback as to the effectiveness of the program.

Dr. John Ozmun, Indiana State University; Dr. Alan Mikesky, Indiana University Medical Center; Dr. David Gallahue, Indiana University; and Dr. Paul Juris, Beth Israel Hospital—my four-person information highway—who gave me access to important academic resources and research.

Glenn "Doc" Rivers, Patrick Ewing, and Derek Harper, who deserve special thanks for their continual encouragement, confidence, and participation that helped make this book a reality.

Finally, to the one man who has had the biggest influence on my past competitive career, as well as my present coaching philosophy. Whenever confronted with a difficult task I ask myself, "What would Dad do in this situation?" An answer always presents itself—one that usually works. Dean Brittenham, my father and mentor, is the standard by which all strength and conditioning coaches are measured. Thanks, Dad, for providing the foundation from which this book was written.

INTRODUCTION

Basketball has had its share of great players. Jabbar with his sky hook. Dr. J with his acrobatic slam dunks. Larry Bird with his incredible court sense and shooting ability. Magic with his extraordinary passes. Tremendous players. All of them able to dominate the action, draw the attention of every fan, and set a new standard of excellence because of a rare combination of physical talent and well-honed basketball skills.

One player in the entire history of the sport, however, stands apart because of his superior "total package." Gliding from one end of the court to the other, dunking from the free-throw line, swiping away an opponent's shot, or rising effortlessly above a defender to release a spectacular jumper, Michael Jordan has allowed us to see what's possible when incomparable physical ability is combined with exceptional basketball skills. He has demonstrated the "total package."

Compare this to a young high school player. Lets say rising star Johnny Dunk is a player who has a respectable vertical jump. In fact, Johnny can dunk the ball from the front of the circle, 9 feet horizontal to the basket. If you were to watch both Johnny and Michael perform the same "monster" dunk, in flight, they would look very similar. The difference between Michael and Johnny would not be the performance of the skill but rather the *level* at which the skill would be performed. The skill itself would be the same. But Michael's "take-off" point would be 6 feet further back than Johnny's: quite a difference!

Johnny's ambition is to perform the *basketball-specific skill* of dunking the ball on the same level as Michael. What training approach should he follow to accomplish this lofty goal? Should Johnny continue to jump from the 9 foot mark and hope that eventually he will be able to "take-off" from the 15 foot line? It will never happen. Should Johnny move back to the 15 foot line and just keep jumping until he makes it? He will never make it. Johnny needs to improve himself as an athlete. He needs to implement a program that will develop *all* the components of athleticism. As Johnny's athletic ability increases, his basketball-specific skills will likewise be raised to new heights.

The idea for this book originated from years of observing athletes from a variety of sports. Many of these athletes would spend endless hours practicing the skills unique to their sport, yet they would realize only limited gains in performance. Have you ever watched a "shooting" practice where a player rarely, if ever, missed a 15 foot jumper? Or where a tennis player returned crushing forehands and backhands against a ball machine? Or where a wide receiver has hands like glue when the defense is *off* the field? During a controlled situation, such as practice, it is easy to exhibit "all pro" skills. But what happens to the 15 foot jumper if the player cannot elude the defense to get an open shot? The tennis player may have the best forehand and backhand in the world, but if she can't get to the ball, who's going to see it? How often will the wide receiver catch the ball if he can't "shake" the cornerback? Most conventional training programs are based on the assumption that if you practice *basketball skills* (e.g., shooting, dribbling, passing, etc.) all other variables involved in the sport will likewise be enhanced. This misconception, unfortunately, dominates the majority of basketball training regimens at all levels. While improving and refining a player's basketball skills is crucial for enhancing the quality of play, it is the improvement of the player's athletic skills that allows him to elevate his play to a higher level.

Athletic skills include variables such as speed, power, endurance, agility, coordination, balance, and reaction time. Improving these athletic skills is critical to the *total development* of the athlete. The level at which basketball skills are performed is directly related to the level of the athlete's *total conditioning*.

As an athlete and a coach for the past 20 years, I can appreciate the incredible complexity of the human body and mind, and I have come to the realization that each of us has only scratched the surface of our physical and mental potential. The human body was created with an almost unlimited capacity for improvement.

Everything that man has created will eventually wear out with use. Your car, television, washing machine, even this book will inevitably deteriorate. The human body is not a machine, but rather an intricate and complex living system. When appropriately challenged, the human body will adapt and become stronger. Unlike man-made machines, the more the body is used, the stronger it becomes and, theoretically, the longer it will last. Conditioning is a process that must be continuous to insure development. Experience indicates that progressive training is instrumental in helping the player to achieve a full measure of improved athleticism.

The new model of the basketball player is one who is a highly conditioned athlete, possessing refined athletic skills, which ultimately elevate the level at which he or she plays the game. Conditioning is the key to consistency in season long, high level performance. Many athletes can boast of isolated games where everything "clicked," and for a brief moment they performed an "all star" *move, shot, pass*, or *dunk* to rival Michael Jordan. However, Michael has done it game after game. In a word, he has *consistency*. Players who are involved in a well-planned conditioning program early in their careers are at a distinct advantage in maximizing potential and limiting the risk of injury. This book will give the coach and/or athlete a means to that end. The text section provides the reader with a *basic* understanding of the physiological principles involved in playing basketball. Following the text are specific drills that illustrate methods to enhance athletic characteristics.

The present state of basketball instruction requires more than just tossing out a ball and playing games. Because of the present high level of play, there is a demand for individuals who have the most up-to-date information about the physical preparation of the athlete. My purpose is not to provide an exhaustive resource on basketball training (for that, I'd have to write a detailed reference book), but to give the reader a basic understanding of the principles involved in improving athletic skills and in planning a safe and effective conditioning program for the athlete. **The primary focus of this book is to provide specific "on-court" activities that develop the movement patterns and energy system for skillfully playing the game of basketball.**

Most books and educators promote the outdated belief that, for a coach to improve fitness among players, he or she must expend considerable time and energy. The simplicity of this program may surprise you. The drills outlined in this book can be easily incorporated into *any* existing practice routine. There are no gimmicks to improving one's basketball conditioning. The instructions in this book will provide athletes and coaches with the tools necessary to improve the level at which they or their athletes perform basketball skills.

CHAPTER 1

FITNESS BASICS FOR BASKETBALL

In sports, the level of specific skill performance separates a champion from the rest of the field. In basketball, the better a player can dribble, shoot, and pass, the better his or her chance of success. But those sport-specific skills are minimized if the player is in poor physical condition.

Refining basketball skills will only get you so far unless you also develop the physical base for performing those skills repeatedly, against physical opponents, throughout the course of a game and season. Thousands of high school and college players can shoot and dribble as well as some pros; however, they typically fall short of the pros in conditioning or athleticism. By that I mean they lack the speed, power, agility, coordination, strength, and endurance needed to compete against players on a higher level. In *Complete Conditioning for Basketball*, I'll show you how to maximize your athleticism through proper physical training.

FITNESS VERSUS ATHLETICISM

Many coaches and players equate athleticism with physical fitness. Being physically fit is not only essential from a health standpoint, but the following components of fitness are equally important for the serious basketball player:

- Cardiorespiratory fitness
- Muscular strength
- Muscular endurance
- Flexibility
- Body composition

For an athlete, however, maintaining a physical capacity beyond the basic standards for health and wellness is critical to insure a high level of performance for an extended period of time. Unfortunately, many pro players who appear to be in great shape pay too little attention to their physical, mental, social, and emotional health, and then wonder why their playing careers are cut short.

While fitness is an indicator of overall health, it is athleticism that determines the level at which sport-specific skills are performed, and athleticism is an indispensable trait among the future stars of the NBA. I'll explain more about how you can develop your athleticism for basketball throughout the book. But first things first. In this chapter we'll look at basic fitness principles and their implications for basketball players.

Cardiorespiratory Fitness

Cardiorespiratory fitness refers to the effectiveness with which the heart (cardio) and lungs (respiratory) deliver blood, oxygen, and nutrients to active body tissue during physical work. Aerobic exercise improves cardiorespiratory function. It also strengthens the heart muscle, improves total cholesterol to HDL ratios, and helps prevent heart disease.

Aerobic training can be done through any activity requiring continuous use of large muscle groups (e.g., walking, running, jogging, swimming, bicycling, cross-country skiing, rowing, etc.) for 20 to 60 minutes, 3 to 5 days per week, at a moderate intensity. Such a training program will improve or maintain your cardiorespiratory fitness. An effectively

trained cardiorespiratory system is capable of sustaining low-intensity effort for a long time because it's capable of consuming vast amounts of oxygen, transporting the oxygen, and aerobically utilizing the oxygen as an energy source for an extended period.

Basketball, on the other hand, requires short and intense periods of activity, so players expend a great deal of energy at a rapid rate. *Anaerobic* pathways are another aspect of cardiorespiratory fitness, and provide energy for high-intensity activities, thus the anaerobic energy systems must also be well developed. Yet even players with excellent anaerobic fitness can go full speed for only so long before having to back off.

Later I'll discuss the respective roles of aerobic and anaerobic fitness and how to train each of these energy paths for effective basketball performance.

Energy Systems for Basketball

The physiology behind the aerobic and anaerobic energy systems is complex. Yet it's important to have a basic understanding of what's involved in order to maximize your own training.

The energy we get from the food we eat is eventually broken down to a chemical compound called *adenosine triphosphate* or *ATP*. Muscle cells use this ATP molecule as the direct and primary energy source for muscle activity.

One source of ATP energy is called *ATP-PC* (phosphocreatine), which is stored within and used directly by the muscle. ATP-PC energy stores last about 10 seconds, and are used when muscles are working maximally, primarily during a quick explosive effort.

A second way of making more ATP available for muscle activity is through anaerobic glycolysis, also referred to as the lactic acid system. In glycolysis, muscle glycogen and blood glucose (both carbohydrates) are broken down (metabolized to a form of usable energy) to produce ATP at an extremely high rate. Both the ATP-PC and glycolysis systems are anaerobic, indicating that they do not require oxygen.

Glycolysis allows the muscle to continue working at a very high intensity but results in the formation of lactic acid (lactate) in the muscle and blood. The accumulation of lactate begins to slow down anaerobic glycolysis and hastens the onset of fatigue, usually within 3 minutes of high-intensity exercise. As a result, exercise must be stopped or its intensity reduced to facilitate the removal and absorption of lactate from the blood and tissue. This leads to the third energy source for the production of ATP, the aerobic system.

The aerobic system, supplying long-term energy, depends on the presence of oxygen for the production of ATP. This is the preferred energy source for exercise longer than 2 or 3 minutes.

When a player begins exercising, all three energy systems (i.e., the ATP-PC, glycolysis, and aerobic systems) are involved. However, the relative contribution of each energy source varies according to the demands of the exercise, which in turn vary as functions of the intensity and duration of the activity (see Table 1.1). Basketball is about 20% aerobic and 80% anaerobic; many factors, however, influence the exact energy expenditure ratio for individual players. For example, some players continually move to "get open," whereas others "fight" for a post-up position; some players inbound the ball, whereas others sprint the floor. Moreover, if we examine the total energy demands for an entire 2-hour game, we find the percent contribution of the energy systems changes continually.

Table 1.1   Energy Systems

Anaerobic/ATP-PC	Anaerobic Glycolysis	Aerobic
(0-10 seconds)	(10 seconds-3 minutes)	(>3 minutes)
*Break-away lay-up	*Continues transitions	*Duration of the game

Assigning exact ratios that would be specific to all styles of play would be impossible. It is widely accepted that basketball is a game requiring a high-level of anaerobic fitness. This is certainly the case when a 2-hour game is broken down into shorter segments. For example, if we were to monitor one person who played all 12 minutes during one quarter, we would see that the ratio of work to rest that the player experienced was 1:1 or less. If we tracked the same player for the entire game, however, assuming he or she played every minute, we would see a work-rest ratio ranging from 1:1 to 1:3 because that game would include short bursts of intense activity virtually unseparated by rest to extended periods of inactivity, such as time-outs, quarter breaks, and half-time breaks. Whereas the energy to perform high-intensity efforts was derived primarily from the *anaerobic* systems during the activity, recovery for subsequent bouts of exercise was facilitated during the periods of rest by the *aerobic* system, via the replenishment of ATP.

You should address all systems in designing an individual training regimen. And, in order to train all three energy systems, you must carefully control the work-rest ratio because that ratio determines which energy system is being trained.

Although the body doesn't select one energy system exclusively over another during exercise, it does favor particular fuel sources, depending on the intensity and duration of the activity. The exact energy system training regimen you'll need depends on your team's style of play (e.g., fastbreak or half-court offense, full-court, man-to-man defensive pressure or zone defense), your position, and your amount of playing time. Later I will discuss why you should vary the work-rest ratio during training to prepare for performing at maximum intensity over a longer duration.

Understanding the concept of the work-rest ratio is important in organizing a training program which specifically stresses the energy system required to play basketball. Within 20 seconds of rest, 50% of the muscles' stores of ATP-PC is restored, and 87% are restored after 60 seconds. The heavy breathing that a player experiences immediately following an explosive short duration (less that 3 minutes) high-intensity activity is called *oxygen debt*. This is the process by which the aerobic system is metabolizing the lactate in an attempt to facilitate rapid recovery. Obviously, a player's ability to tolerate high accumulation levels of lactate will delay the onset of fatigue and enhance productivity on the court.

While the body does not select one energy system exclusively over another during exercise, it does have preferred fuel sources given the intensity and duration of the activity. The exact energy system training regimen you'll need depends on your team's style of play (e.g., fastbreak versus half-court offense, full court man-to-man defensive pressure versus zone defense, etc.), your position, and your amount of playing time.

Muscular Strength

From the high school level on up, the modern game of basketball requires strength—the ability to generate and exert maximal force. Today's player must be ready for contact. Successful players are sufficiently muscled to drive strong to the hoop, get shots off after being fouled, post up, "fight" through and set picks, and establish rebounding position. Adequate strength also helps in the prevention of injuries and is a very important fitness component. I will discuss developing muscular strength in chapters 3 and 4.

Regular participation in a strength training program that is tailored to your specific strength and conditioning needs will add muscle to your game. Patrick Ewing, Karl Malone, Anthony Mason, and Kevin Willis are just a few of the many NBA players whose enhanced strength has allowed them to raise their game to the next level.

Muscular Endurance

Muscular endurance is the ability of a muscle or group of muscles to contract and exert force repeatedly over an extended period of time.

Players who "lose their legs" at the end of a game are probably suffering from inadequate muscular endurance. You've probably experienced this yourself, if not during a game, then during a lengthy practice. Your legs have no more "spring." Fresher and better conditioned players are blowing by you on the fast break, and you feel like you're moving in slow motion.

When Doc Rivers was rehabing from his 1994 season-ending injury, one of the things that shocked him was how quickly he became fatigued from simple, everyday activities. There he was, a professional athlete "winded" after walking up one flight of stairs. Through low resistance and progressively longer exercise sessions, Doc was able to regain his muscular endurance and his stamina. Once his strength and conditioning base was re-established, he was able to incorporate higher intensity activities into his training regimen.

I'll discuss developing muscular endurance at greater length in chapter 3.

Flexibility

The ability to move joints throughout their full range of motion free of discomfort and pain is an important part of fitness and athleticism. Muscle suppleness and good joint mobility are often associated with efficient and coordinated movement.

It's easy to see then why good flexibility is essential for effective basketball performance. Whether crouching in a defensive stance or throwing a length-of-the-court pass, a player must have sufficient joint flexibility. In addition, maintaining good flexibility can decrease the incidence and severity of injury in the event a muscle is subjected to an extreme stress.

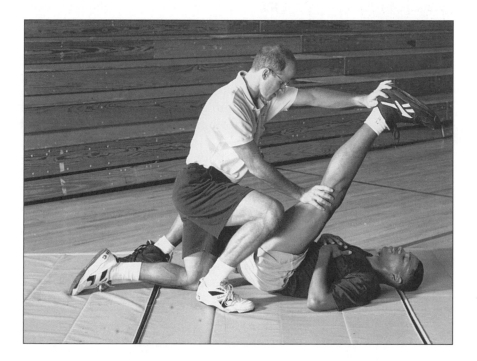

A proper stretching regimen will promote adequate flexibility. From a fitness standpoint, a simple 10-minute stretching routine in the morning and again at night can produce very positive results. Muscles will be less tense during the work day and joints should be less stiff when you get out of bed in the morning.

Basketball players should also stretch prior to practice and games, **after** muscles have been warmed up by jogging, calisthenics, low-intensity shooting drills, and so on. Stretching will help prepare the body for the exertion that follows. And stretching immediately following a practice or game will help your body recover from the stressful activity and maintain or increase joint range of motion. I'll present more on flexibility, including some suggested stretches for basketball players, in chapter 2.

Body Composition

Several components make up your body's total mass. Body composition refers to a person's relative amounts of fat and lean body mass. Normal ranges for the percentage of fat in the body make-up are 8% to 13% for *athletic* males and 16% to 20% for *athletic* females. For basketball players, the ideal range should be less. However, players who persistently measure in the low end of the range may need professional dietary counseling to get back to a more normal percentage of body fat.

Overweight does not necessarily mean overfat. *Obesity* refers to having too much fat, and often, but not always, coincides with being overweight. On the basketball court, an obese player is endangering his or her health by having to lug around excess fat weight. This player is more susceptible to fatigue and injury; quite possibly the player's athleticism and basketball skill performance will be adversely affected as well.

Whether or not you have to worry about your weight or percent body fat, you should, like all basketball players, always practice good nutritional habits. In addition to supplying your body with the basic energy it needs, a proper diet will help you stay healthy, build muscle, and perform maximally on the court.

Less Fat Contributes to Better Results

On my first day as the Knicks strength and conditioning coach, I took some anthropometric measures of our point guard, Mark Jackson (at the time of this writing, Mark is with the Indiana Pacers). Mark weighed 199 pounds and his body fat was 15.7%. Mark's higher-than-desired body fat percentage was reflected in his test scores:

- 20-yard dash = 3.31 seconds
- Vertical jump = 27.5 inches
- Agility run = 4.92 seconds

With the help of a very intense conditioning program focused on strength, power, speed, and nutritional counseling, Mark was able to reduce his body fat to 8.6% in just 6 months. And, not coincidentally, Mark's test scores improved dramatically:

- 20-yard dash =2.91 seconds
- Vertical jump = 30.5 inches
- Agility run = 4.44 seconds

These improvements cannot be attributed solely to a lower percentage of body fat. Mark's motivation to improve as a total athlete had a lot to do with it. And as a result he had one of his most productive years of his basketball career.

CONDITIONING PRINCIPLES

A working knowledge of the physiological principles involved in basketball training and competition is extremely valuable for players and coaches. It will help you take a more informed and active role in planning, customizing, and adjusting a training program to produce maximum results for *you*.

Specificity

We're now moving beyond the realm of basic fitness conditioning and into more sophisticated sport-specific training concepts. It's not enough to be well-conditioned; you must hone your body specifically for basketball. If you want to improve your free throw shooting, what do you do? Play golf? No. You shoot free throws. *Many* free throws. The same rationale applies to your physical conditioning. Through specific adaptation, the body changes metabolically and/or mechanically (movement skill) in response to a specific demand. An athlete may be well conditioned, but is he or she conditioned to play the game of basketball? And that's the premise of specificity of training.

As mentioned earlier, basketball is primarily an anaerobic sport that also places demands on the aerobic system. Training specifically for basketball, therefore, means using a regimen that stresses anaerobic energy production. In order to improve the capacity of these energy pathways you should perform short-term, high-intensity exercises. The court conditioning drills provided in chapters 8 and 9 are the perfect choice.

Not only do the court drills stress the anaerobic energy system, many of them incorporate athletic skills such as speed, quickness, agility, acceleration, deceleration, and a variety of movement patterns a player will encounter during the course of a game; total training specifically for basketball.

Adaptation

Physiological responses to training are very predictable. If the body is carefully and progressively challenged, adaptations will occur and the body will become stronger. This is the concept of progressive overload. When the body experiences a physical stress, as long as the stress is not too severe, the body will "adapt" to that stress. For example, adaptation may include muscle growth (hypertrophy) following repeated bouts of resistance training or improved cardiorespiratory efficiency following aerobic exercise.

As the fitness level increases, so does your capacity to work harder and longer.

Conversely, a period of inactivity that causes a decline in physical capacity will adversely affect your fitness and performance. For example, if you take a long vacation during the off-season and do little or no training, you'll experience a detraining effect. Your body responds just like an arm that has been in a cast for several months. Its physical capacity declines; it loses its vitality.

By staying in shape you can get the most out of your physical potential. More importantly, whether it is pre-, post-, or in-season, if you're well-conditioned you'll be less susceptible to injury or minimize the severity of the problem should an injury occur. So maintaining a good conditioning base will work to your advantage if a long and successful basketball career is in your plans.

To achieve an optimal level of physical stress, keep in mind the progressive overload principle. As your fitness level improves, you should gradually increase the intensity of the physical stress you are imposing on your body. The three major variables in determining appropriate stress are intensity, frequency, and duration. When you manipulate these variables intelligently, you can produce the fitness and performance outcomes you're after.

Intensity

Intensity is probably the most important of the three factors. Intensity of a training session can be measured by both the *degree of difficulty* and by *time considerations*. Given the anaerobic nature of basketball, most exertion takes place in short bursts, with brief stops in between. The conditioning exercises and drills in this book are tailored to these anaerobic energy needs of high-intensity work for 3 minutes or less.

The aerobic system also needs attention. An efficient aerobic system will help the body better tolerate increases in lactate level, facilitate lactate removal, and enhance the speed of recovery. This will, in turn, allow a player to perform maximally for longer durations.

To develop a solid aerobic base, engage in continuous activity at a submaximal effort for 20 to 60 minutes. You can still use the drills to work your aerobic system. Simply decrease the intensity, execute the drills over a longer duration, and shorten the rest interval between sets. A simple way to determine intensity is to monitor the heart rate. If you're able to carry on a conversation while maintaining a target heart rate of 65% to 90% of your predicted maximal heart rate, that's a good indicator of submaximal effort. For a rough estimate to predict maximal heart rate (within 10 beats per minute), simply subtract your age from 220. For example, a 17-year-old player would have a predicted maximal heart rate of 203 (220 − 17 = 203).

Now let's say that the same athlete wants to train at 70% of his or her maximal heart rate. Simply multiply 203 x 70%, which equals 142.1. This means that the athlete should achieve and maintain a heart rate of approximately 142 beats per minute during the training session.

Another method of calculating your predicted maximal heart rate (theoretically more accurate) is the Karvonen formula. This method uses *maximal heart rate* and *resting heart rate* to determine the *heart rate reserve* (see Table 1.2).

Whichever method you use, the value of knowing your target heart rate and/or heart rate reserve is critical for regulating the intensity of

Table 1.2 Determining Your Target Heart Rate

(Assuming a training intensity level of 70% Heart Rate Reserve)

220– _____ = _____ Predicted Maximal Heart Rate
       Your Age

_____ – _____ = _____

Predicted Maximal HR   Resting HR   Heart Rate Reserve

_____ x .70 = _____ + _____ = THR at 70%

   HR Reserve   Resting HR   HR Reserve

your training at the appropriate level. Aerobic training such as this should be considered an important component of an early off-season program. Late off-season, pre-season, and in-season training should consist primarily of anaerobic activity.

During anaerobic exercise, the heart rate will typically rise to 95% of maximum or higher. And heart rates of 180 beats per minute are common among healthy athletes engaged in anaerobic training. Obviously, a work rate of this intensity cannot be sustained for long. Unfortunately, a lot of players quickly learn to pace themselves during particularly demanding workouts. An occasional heart rate check immediately following a drill will determine if they are putting forth maximal effort. Since the anaerobic system supplies most of the energy for intense work lasting up to 2 to 3 minutes, during training the intensity of repetitions and sets should be based on a 3 minute *or less* maximal effort. As a general rule, a rest break of only 30 seconds following a 2-minute maximal effort will not adequately remove accumulated lactate from the muscles and blood, whereas a rest break of greater than 2 minutes will allow for a significantly greater recovery of the energy required to perform the next work interval at the desired intensity. If you take a longer break, your subsequent efforts should be at or near maximal intensity.

Many times I have shortened the rest interval and sacrificed maximal effort for the positive training adaptation that results from tolerating high levels of lactate buildup. (Experiencing discomfort from accumulated lactate is not uncommon during a game, so players may as well get used to it!)

During conditioning drills, players often miss more shots than during practice time. Coaches should remember that, as the intensity of a drill increases, coordination and accuracy decrease. While missing shots during a conditioning drill should not be encouraged, the coach should remain aware of the activity's purpose. Intensity and rest must be directed toward the player's needs and approximate the requirements of playing basketball. And remember, the intensity of the exercises largely determines whether or not the emphasis of the energy system being trained is anaerobic or aerobic. Exercise intensity and work-rest ratio will vary dramatically depending upon the time of year.

Duration

Duration is largely dependent upon intensity and refers to the *length* of a training session. If the intensity of a drill is high, then the duration will likely be short. Similarly, a low-to-moderate level of intensity would dictate a longer duration.

As you develop your fitness you'll be able to recover more quickly after short intense periods of activity. Say that you're playing a running and pressing team and go more than 2 minutes straight, all-out, up and down the court before play is stopped. If you're in good shape, you'll be able to recover during a time-out and return to the court refreshed. If your conditioning is weaker, you'll not have enough time during the brief rest period to remove a significant amount of lactate, and you will rapidly fatigue.

Unlike a marathon runner who functions at a slow, steady pace for more than 2 hours and relies almost solely on aerobic energy, you'll be working more intensely, accelerating, decelerating, jumping, and cutting throughout 2-plus hours on the court. So duration has a double-meaning for you: (a) How long you go during any given stretch of a game, practice, or drill without rest; and (b) the total length of your participation in a game or practice session.

Frequency

Frequency refers to *how often* you train or play over a given period of time. Positive results from training are achieved when stress is applied at an appropriate level of intensity, for a predetermined duration, several times (adjusted seasonally) per week. Based on the principle of progressive overload, if the stress is of appropriate intensity, duration, and frequency, then training improvements will occur. In other words, the body will adapt positively to the new demands you're placing on it.

A couple of important points to keep in mind pertaining to adaptation and frequency are that (a) the adaptation will be specific to the stress, and that (b) all physiological adaptation will occur during recovery. Therefore, rest is an essential part of your conditioning program. Not just rest between sets **within** a workout session, but rest **between** sessions and seasons.

During the off-season and pre-season, schedule a minimum of two or three court conditioning workouts per week (not on consecutive days). That's the fewest workouts you can do and still realize gains in your anaerobic fitness. In-season, when you're playing two to four games a week, you should do anaerobic training only 1 or 2 days a week.

Periodization

Periodization is the organized training of an athlete or a team throughout the year culminating in an optimal level of conditioning and/or performance at a designated time in the season. Basketball is a sport in which every game counts, and training through the season in order to peak during the playoffs is unrealistic. Therefore a systematic training regimen provides fluctuations in (a) training intensity (the degree of difficulty of an exercise; the quality of work), (b) volume (the quantity of work), and (c) technique (athletic and basketball skills) implemented to maximize the training effect and ultimately elevate performance.

All training variables can be manipulated, including strength training, basketball skills, and the drills outlined in this book. Table 1.3 is a simple yearly plan based on the variables of intensity, volume, and technique for the various seasons. By manipulating these variables, you can effectively prepare for the coming season.

Progression

Because you'll be experiencing fitness gains, you'll need to adjust your training frequently to insure further improvement. Remember the concept of progressive overload.

Determining the appropriate intensity of training is a constant challenge to any basketball coach or athlete. First, you must start at a work level that you can handle easily. This will ensure a degree of success and help develop confidence in your training. Then the intensity should be gradually increased to progressively raise your fitness level. Too much too soon and you run the risk of soreness, injury, and disappointment. Too little too late, and your fitness will plateau and you'll probably get bored with the program and eventually quit altogether. In either case, you won't be in shape to perform up to your potential on the basketball court.

Table 1.3   Periodization Schedule

	Off-season	First half pre-season	Second half pre-season	Transition of 1-2 weeks: Basket-ball-specific active rest	Regular season	Post season	Transition of 2-4 weeks: Player's choice of active rest
Intensity	Low	Low/Mod.	Mod./High		Mod./High	High	
Volume	High	Mod./High	Low/Mod.		Moderate	Low	
Technique	Low	Low/Mod.	Moderate		Mod./High	High	

Additional Keys to Basketball Conditioning

Not all of the important training you need to do is physical, on-court activity. To support a "total training" philosophy, you also need plenty of rest, a good diet, and a fitness mind-set.

Rest

In order for your body to receive the full benefits from a training program, you must allow for ample rest and recovery. Not only rest between specific exercises within a workout, but rest between training sessions, and rest between training phases (seasons). By rest I am not simply referring to sleep, although 6 to 8 hours of shut-eye a night is recommended for most athletes. Rest also applies to the days you don't train, train at a very low intensity, or cross-train. Whenever you allow a strained energy system, muscle group, or body part to recover, you're resting it.

Remember that physical adaptation to stress occurs during rest. It is during the rest interval that your body "rebuilds" in preparation for subsequent effort. So appropriate rest insures that the training effect will be maximized. If you are a training "fanatic" and you do not allow your body to recover between training sessions, you will often experience plateaus, or even a decline in your conditioning level.

How do you avoid such setbacks? It's not enough to have a great daily exercise routine: you must also evaluate the effectiveness of each workout for symptoms of overtraining. Monitor such signs as difficulty recovering from a particularly demanding training session; muscle soreness that persists beyond 48 hours post-exercise; chronic pain in the joints; disrupted sleep and/or fatigue following sleep; extreme changes in normal bodily functions; lack of motivation; lethargy; and depression. If you notice any of these symptoms, adjust the intensity, duration, and frequency of your workouts, and continue to observe any changes. Include a day or two per week devoted strictly to rest. Go for a leisurely walk, ride a bicycle, play some tennis or golf. In other words, stay active, but get away from the daily grind.

In the Periodization Schedule (p.17), you'll notice a couple of "active rest" periods that follow the pre-season and regular (or post-) season. As with the rest between exercises within a session, and rest between sessions within a training phase, the rest between training phases is equally important to insure maximal adaptation and minimal overuse syndrome. During these 1 to 4 week periods, your activity should remain intense—but the duration and frequency of that activity should drop considerably. Rest is essential for preventing fatigue and injury and promoting growth. In training, you have to be alert to the signs of fatigue and adjust workouts accordingly.

The Importance of Rest

Knicks player Derek Harper's experience confirms the importance of rest for preventing fatigue and injury and promoting growth. His approach toward conditioning was extreme: he had to be convinced that training 4 hours a day, 7 days a week could be harmful to his health. It wasn't until he adopted prescribed rest and recovery intervals (a) throughout the workout, (b) between sessions, and (c) following seasons, that Derek began to obtain the full benefits of his hard work. In Derek's words, "Even at age 33, and after 12 years in the NBA, I can honestly say that I am in the best physical condition of my entire career. All aspects of my conditioning have improved—speed, strength, and endurance the most dramatically."

Nutrition

Early onset fatigue in games or practice can often be linked to poor dietary habits. A high-energy diet consisting mostly of carbohydrate should be your fuel of choice. During a typical 2-hour practice, you can use up most of your carbohydrate energy supply. So it is important that after practice you replenish the carbohydrate stores in preparation for your next workout or game. Maintaining good eating habits *throughout the year*, not just on game day or during the season, will bring you closer to optimal health and maximize your physical potential.

Carbohydrate.   Carbohydrate can be classified as either complex or simple. The chemical makeup of complex carbohydrate provides a prolonged release of energy, making a steady supply of energy available for a long time. Complex carbohydrate found in foods such as root vegetables, breads, whole grain cereals, beans, and pasta, should be your main source of calories. Simple carbohydrate such as sugar, honey, candies, and jellies creates a rapid but temporary rush of energy followed by low blood sugar, which robs the athlete of both energy and intensity and can negatively affect performance. Among simple carbohydrate fructose is an exception which can be found in fruits, juices, and vegetables. Because of its chemical composition, fructose provides an immediate source of energy, yet it does not rapidly lower blood sugar. Foods containing fructose are typically excellent sources of other important nutrients, such as vitamins, minerals, and fiber.

To maximize your training and better prepare you for practice sessions and competition, choose a high-energy diet consisting of 60% to 70% carbohydrate.

Fat.   Fat is a tremendous source of concentrated energy, providing more than twice the calories per gram that carbohydrates or protein do. Energy from fat is used only after the available energy (supplied primarily from carbohydrate) has been depleted: It takes about 30 minutes of exercise to reach this point. Because of the game's explosive nature, basketball will use glycogen as the major fuel, but in a typical game of 2 to 2-1/2 hours, fat will contribute somewhat to the overall energy. This does not give you the green light to freely indulge in fat consumption. On the contrary, most nutritional experts recommend that fat consumption for the athlete should not exceed 15% to 25% of the total caloric intake. High fat diets have been linked to cardiovascular diseases, cancers, and hypertension. Red meat, poultry, fish, salad dressings, margarine, butter, dairy products, eggs, nuts, seeds, and certain vegetables and fruits are sources of fat.

Protein.   Second only to water as the most abundant substance in the body, protein is essential for tissue growth and repair. Eight of the proteins necessary for health cannot be produced by the body, and must be acquired daily through diet. Meats contain all eight of these "essential" proteins, but meat is a poor energy source; usually contains a lot of fat; and is sometimes difficult to digest. To reduce your consumption of animal protein you can add grains, nuts, seeds, legumes, and other vegetables to your diet. Although these sources each lack one or more of the essential amino acids, by combining them with limited servings of animal products, you should have no problem meeting the daily requirement for protein. However, if your diet consists of very little meat or if you're a strict vegetarian, you should consult with a registered dietitian to be certain that you are eating the appropriate combinations of essential amino acids.

Many athletes mistakenly believe that consuming excessive amounts of protein will contribute to massive growth of muscles. Eating even 10 to 15 times the recommended amount is not uncommon. Although athletes do require slightly higher amounts of protein than sedentary people, their protein intake should not exceed 15% to 18% of their total caloric consumption. As with carbohydrate and fat, the body can use only a limited amount of protein: the excess will be converted to and stored as fat.

Vitamins and Minerals.   Vitamins are critical to the metabolism of food. Carbohydrate, fat, and protein will be of limited value without vitamins. Minerals are most often associated with the hard structures of the body, such as bones and teeth. Although the body's concentrations of minerals are extremely minute, they serve a vital role in many body functions. Diets that include a wide variety of fruits, vegetables, and low fat protein sources (especially complex carbohydrate) usually provide all the vitamins and minerals necessary to maintain an active life. Consuming large doses of vitamin and mineral supplements is of little value, and in some extreme instances these supplements can actually create chemical imbalances that are quite toxic. If you feel you must bolster your diet with vitamin and mineral supplements, it is important to discuss your nutritional needs with a doctor or registered dietitian.

Water.   The single most important variable affecting performance is water consumption. Sweating, respiration, urination, and other body processes can greatly disrupt an athlete's water balance. It doesn't take much to do this. From a water loss of merely 2 pounds, the athlete may experience as much as a 15% decrease in physical capacity. And it is not uncommon for athletes to lose 5 pounds of water in a single game or training session! Too often, I've seen a player hit the wall midway through the fourth quarter not for lack of conditioning but because of inadequate fluid consumption. To prevent the ill effects of dehydration, we require that each Knicks player drink 10 ounces of fluid every 30 minutes, whether or not he feels thirsty.

There is a time lag between the need for fluid replacement and the feeling of thirst. To avoid dehydration, therefore, you should drink 2 to 3 cups of water 1 hour before competition, whether or not you feel thirsty. Drink another 1 or 2 cups 10 to 20 minutes before tip-off and continue to drink 1/2 to 1 cup every 20 to 30 minutes throughout the game or practice. Cool water (40-50 degrees) will be absorbed faster and will not cause cramping. Drink at least six 8-ounce glasses of water daily. You need that much just to properly maintain normal body functions.

Power Eating for Games or Workouts

Pre-Game	Game	Post-Game
EAT some protein, minimal fat, and liberal amounts of carbohydrate.	EAT very little at half time; if you must, choose from yogurt, breads, graham crackers, high carbohydrate energy bar.	EAT same as pre-game, emphasizing fruits, grains, pasta, etc.
DRINK two-three 8-oz glasses of water 1-2 hours before game or practice; one-two 8-oz glasses 10-20 minutes before tip-off.	DRINK 1/2-1 cup water or fruit juice every 20-30 minutes.	DRINK several cups water or fruit juice.
AVOID meats, fried foods, added fats (butter, mayonnaise, oily salad dressings, etc.), sugary foods and drinks.	AVOID sugary drinks or "sports" drinks, fats, and other heavy foods.	AVOID fatty meats, eggs, fried foods.

Fitness Mind-Set

Most of us have some idea of how to improve strength, speed, power, and conditioning, but what about our minds? Is our mind-set really that important to successful performance?

Do not underestimate the power of your mind. Tapping the unlimited potential of the human brain unleashes a tremendous mental advantage in a conditioning process. Concentration, creativity, memory, motivation, and mental processing all have a role to play in competition. Think of the importance of psyching up prior to meeting your crosstown rival, of mental imagery as you stand at the free-throw line, or of stress management during the closing seconds of a tie ball game. All of these mental activities are critical to the successful basketball player. Although the mental aspect of playing basketball isn't the focus of this text, it is nonetheless a crucial component of total training.

The information I've provided in this chapter and in the rest of *Complete Conditioning for Basketball* should help you take control and make the most of your potential for fitness, athleticism, and basketball. But without the right mind-set, you cannot use your knowledge to maximum advantage. I encourage you to increase your mental efficacy by continually accepting challenges, confronting unexpected circumstances, acquiring new mental and physical skills, and never losing sight of the enormous capability you have yet to unleash.

CHAPTER 2

FLEXIBILITY

I mentioned in chapter 1 the value of flexibility as a key component for general health and fitness. For the athlete, insuring an adequate *range of motion* is additionally important because it

- allows for efficiency of movement to perform certain skills more effectively,
- decreases the susceptibility to injury, and
- facilitates coordinated movements, which in turn, aid other athletic attributes such as speed, power, and agility.

Stretching is one of the best ways to insure a measure of flexibility. But don't just walk onto the court, sit down, and start stretching. Instead, begin each training session with a 3 to 5 minute warm-up. Stretching without warming up could actually do more harm than good. Many athletes' injuries have resulted from stretching a "cold" muscle. A warm-up and stretching period should become part of your pre-game and pre-practice ritual.

WARM-UP

The best type of basketball warm-up is one that is specific to the needs of the athlete and mimics the movements involved in the sport. The court conditioning drills illustrated in this manual make excellent active warm-ups if they are simply performed at reduced intensity.

The goal of the warm-up is to increase specific muscle and core body temperature. A passive warm-up includes massage, hot hydrotherapy, heating pads, or elevating the body temperature by some other external means. The more preferred active warm-up involves specific muscle or total body movements such as calisthenics, jogging, or practicing basketball skills. A good indicator of the body's rising temperature is the presence of perspiration.

Some of the more obvious physiological changes that occur during an active warm-up include the following:

- *Increased blood flow to the working muscles.* This enhances ATP-PC replenishment because a greater volume of blood in the muscles makes needed energy readily available during physical work. It also decreases blood flow to nonessential areas of the body, in other words, to the muscles that play a limited role in the upcoming activity.

- *Decreased muscle viscosity.* A warmed muscle, saturated with blood, is much more elastic and will facilitate a more powerful contraction with less friction.

- *Improved functioning of nerve transmission.* A slightly elevated muscle temperature enhances the function of the nervous receptors and the speed of the message transmission. This contributes to an increase in the speed of muscle contraction and ultimately an increase in power production.

- *Reduced risk of soft tissue injury.* Most importantly, a warm, fully oxygenated muscle is less prone to injury.

Just think—all of those benefits from just 3 to 5 minutes of light work. Take advantage of this bargain. Your body will thank you.

STRETCHING

Until recently, basketball players spent little time and even less effort improving their flexibility. But coaches and athletes now recognize the many benefits of a simple daily stretching routine. Pat Riley of the Knicks is a strong proponent of warming up and stretching. Coach Riley allows a minimum of 20 minutes and sometimes as much as 40 minutes per practice for warm-up and stretching; and it pays off. For instance, during the '91-'92 season, the Knicks had *zero* soft tissue injuries and the same five starters began every pre-season, regular season, and post-season game.

The methods for increasing flexibility range from the dynamic, sometimes violent, ballistic movements to the more disciplined and passive yoga techniques. The ultimate goal is to improve muscle suppleness. I recommend *static stretching* as a safe and effective method of achieving flexibility. By holding a stretch for 10 seconds (preferably 15-20 seconds) without movement, you are less likely to exceed the extensibility of the muscle, which can result in the tearing of muscle fibers. Static stretching elicits an *inverse stretch reflex* that actually relaxes the muscle, facilitating maximal gains in flexibility.

A committed basketball player should stretch a minimum of 10 to 15 minutes per session, two or three times per day, 7 days per week. Follow these guidelines when you perform the static stretches:

- Stretch to the point of moderate tension and hold for a minimum of 10 seconds (preferably 15-20 seconds).
- Relax for 3 to 5 seconds and repeat. Spend additional time on muscles that are chronically tight.
- Perform two to three sets per stretching exercise (time permitting).
- Stretch in a smooth and controlled manner; avoid fast and bouncy movements.
- Breathe deeply and rhythmically.
- Concentrate on the muscles being stretched.
- Try to make progress every time you stretch.
- Stretch before and after games and workouts.
- Maintain a balance between stretching and strengthening exercises to insure joint stability, which will help minimize the chance of a joint injury.

The 15 basic stretches that follow are well-suited for most basketball players. However, because every athlete has special, individual needs, it's impossible to present an ideal stretching program for all players. Develop a routine that works best for *you*.

ARM CIRCLES

Focus: Muscles of the arm and shoulder region

Procedure: Stand with feet shoulder-width apart, knees slightly flexed. Swing the arms in a large circle from the shoulders, keeping elbows straight. The movement is slow. To begin, reach as high as possible with the left arm (left shoulder should almost touch the left ear). Simultaneously begin moving the left arm forward and down while the right arm moves back and up. As shown below, the right arm is now fully extended above the head (right shoulder should almost touch the right ear).

Duration: Perform 10 to 15 revolutions forward, then backward. For an added challenge, try moving one arm forward while the other arm moves backward (good luck).

SHOULDER STRETCH

Focus: Rear deltoid and surrounding musculature of the shoulder and upper back

Procedure: Stand with feet shoulder-width apart, knees slightly flexed. Extend the left arm across the body. With the right hand positioned just above the left elbow, gently pull the left arm until the stretch is felt in the left shoulder. Turn the head and look to the left. Keep the shoulders square, don't rotate the trunk.

Duration: Hold the stretch for a minimum of 10 seconds. Repeat on the opposite side.

TRICEPS STRETCH

Focus: Triceps (the back of the upper arm)

Procedure: While still standing, extend the left arm over head. Flex the
left elbow and place the palm of the left hand in the middle of the back
(upper left arm should be touching the head). Reach behind the head
and gently apply pressure to the left elbow with the right hand. Push
back and down on the left elbow.

Duration: Hold the stretch for a minimum of 10 seconds. Repeat on the
opposite side.

FOREARM AND WRIST

Focus: Muscles of the lower arm

Procedure: Extend the left arm in front of the body (parallel to the floor). Point the left hand and fingers to the ceiling (see Figure a). Position the palm of the right hand at the base of the fingers of the left hand and gently pull back. Hold this stretch for a minimum of 10 seconds. Now point the fingers of the left hand down to the floor and position the right hand on the big knuckles of the left hand (see Figure b). Again, gently pull back.

Duration: Hold both positions for a minimum of 10 seconds. Repeat on the opposite side.

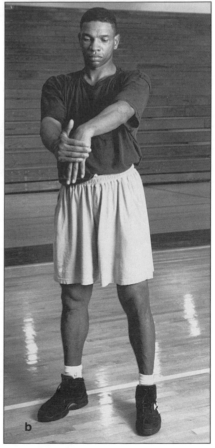

SIDE STRETCH

Focus: Oblique and latissimus muscles (the muscles of the side, upper and lower back)

Procedure: Stand with the feet slightly wider than shoulder-width apart. Flex the knees slightly and point the toes straight ahead. Place the right hand on the right thigh. Reach the left hand overhead and simultaneously slide the right hand down the right leg. Stop when a moderate stretch is felt all along the left side.

Duration: Hold the stretch for a minimum of 10 seconds. Repeat on the opposite side.

HIP FLEXOR

Focus: Hip flexors (the muscles on the front and upper thigh)

Procedure: From the Side Stretch position (p. 30) turn the body to the right. The right leg is in front of the left and both feet are pointed straight ahead. Depending on the level of flexibility, a wider stance may have to be taken for this stretch to be more effective. Place the hands on the hips. With the shoulders back, flex the right (front) leg and drop the upper body (trunk and torso) down toward the floor. Note: the left leg should be fully extended and the athlete's upper body should be perpendicular to the floor.

Duration: Hold the stretch for a minimum of 10 seconds. Repeat on the opposite side.

STANDING "QUAD" STRETCH

Focus: Quadriceps (the muscles on the front of the thigh)

Procedure: Stand on the right leg, right foot pointed to the wall. The right hand is touching the wall. Flex the left knee and grasp the left ankle with the left hand. Don't pull the left foot and ankle in tight; instead, maintain several inches between the foot and buttocks. Keep the upper body and shoulders back—do not lean forward. Point the left knee straight to the ground.

Duration: Hold the stretch for a minimum of 10 seconds. Repeat on the opposite side.

CALF STRETCH

Focus: Upper calf musculature (part 1) and Achilles tendon and lower calf musculature (part 2)

Procedure: *Part 1:* Place the forearms on the wall. Place the left leg and foot (left knee straight), approximately 2 or 3 feet behind the right leg and foot (right knee flexed). Point both feet toward the wall. There should be a straight line between the left shoulder, hip, knee, and ankle (see Figure a). Slowly move the hips forward to intensify the stretch. Hold for a minimum of 10 seconds and proceed with Part 2.

Part 2: From the above position, place the hands on the wall and fully extend the arms. Move the left (back) leg forward several inches closer to the right (front) leg. Keep both feet pointed toward the wall. Flex the left knee. The upper body should be positioned directly above the toes of the left foot (see Figure b). Slowly allow the upper body weight to drop down, intensifying the stretch of the Achilles and lower calf.

Duration: Hold Part 1 position for a minimum of 10 seconds. Then move immediately into Part 2 and hold for another 10 seconds. Repeat on the opposite side.

INVERTED HURDLER'S STRETCH

Focus: Low back, hamstrings, and some upper calf musculature

Procedure: Sit on the floor with the left leg extended in front, and bend the right leg at the knee with the sole of the right foot touching the inside of the extended left leg. Point the left foot to the ceiling. With the left hand, reach across and grab the right (bent) knee. Reach the right arm overhead and toward the left foot. If done correctly, a good stretch along the side and throughout the musculature of the lower back will be felt.

Duration: Hold the stretch for a minimum of 10 seconds. Then, without relaxing the stretch along the low back and side, move immediately to the Inverted Hurdler's Stretch Progression.

INVERTED HURDLER'S STRETCH PROGRESSION

Focus: Hamstrings, low back, and some upper calf musculature

Procedure: From the final position of the Inverted Hurdler's Stretch, turn and reach both arms toward the foot of the extended left leg. Keep the back straight, head up (lean forward from the hips and do not hunch the shoulders).

Duration: Hold the stretch for a minimum of 10 seconds, and immediately move to the Pretzel Stretch.

PRETZEL STRETCH

Focus: The muscles of the spine, hip, and buttocks

Procedure: This is a natural extension from the Inverted Hurdler's Stretch Progression. Sit tall, pick up the bent right leg and cross it over the straight left leg so that the right foot is flat on the floor alongside the left knee. Take the left arm across the body and place the left elbow on the outside of the right knee. Look over the right shoulder and slowly twist the upper body to the right while simultaneously applying force to the right knee with the left elbow.

Duration: Hold the stretch for a minimum of 10 seconds. Now repeat the Inverted Hurdler's Stretch, the Progression, and the Pretzel Stretch to the opposite side.

LOW BACK AND GLUTEUS STRETCH

Focus: The muscles of the low back, upper hamstrings, and gluteus

Procedure: While lying on the back, extend the right leg on the floor. Bend the left leg and grasp *under* the knee with both hands. Gently hug the left leg to the chest. Concentrate on keeping the low back and spine in contact with the floor at all times. Less flexible individuals may want to flex the right knee slightly (keep the right foot on the floor) to insure floor contact for spinal support.

Duration: Hold the stretch for a minimum of 10 seconds. Move on to the Spinal Twist.

Variation: Hug both knees to the chest simultaneously (keep the arms *under* the knees). Remember to keep the entire spine in contact with the floor throughout the duration of the stretch.

SPINAL TWIST

Focus: Gluteus and low back musculature

Procedure: A good progression from the preceding stretch is to take the bent (left) knee across the body toward the floor on the outside of the straight (right) leg. Keep the shoulders flat on the floor and look toward the ceiling.

Duration: Hold the stretch for a minimum of 10 seconds. Repeat the Low Back and Gluteus Stretch and Spinal Twist to the opposite side.

CROSS-LEG GLUTEUS STRETCH

Focus: Gluteus, upper hamstrings, and low back musculature

Procedure: In a supine position, cross the left leg over the right. Position the left ankle on the thigh just below the right knee. Reach the left hand through the left leg, the right hand around the right leg, and grasp *behind* the right knee with both hands. Gently pull the right leg toward the chest. The stretch should be felt on the left leg.

Duration: Hold the stretch for a minimum of 10 seconds and repeat on the opposite side.

BUTTERFLY GROIN STRETCH

Focus: Groin and inner thigh musculature

Procedure: Sit tall with the soles of the feet together, heels close to the buttocks, knees flared out. Keep the back straight, head up. Grab the ankles and lean forward at the hips as if to bring the chest toward the feet. Avoid "fighting" the stretch. Instead concentrate on relaxing the groin muscles. To increase the intensity of the stretch apply downward pressure with the elbows to the knees.

Duration: Hold the stretch for a minimum of 10 seconds and repeat.

COOL-DOWN

At the end of each workout take 5 to 10 minutes to do some low-intensity activity, such as easy jogging followed by a light stretching routine. This cool-down period will help the body to return to its pre-exercise state. It's a small investment of time for the many benefits you'll receive. A properly performed cool-down will

- help clear the muscles of accumulated lactate,
- lessen excessive fatigue,
- reduce soreness and cramps,
- keep muscles from "tightening up,"
- lower blood pressure, and
- drop body temperature back to resting levels.

In short, a cool-down speeds overall recovery in preparation for subsequent workouts or games. It's also simple to do. And many players use it as a way to unwind after practices and games, as a transition from the intensity and business on the court to the more relaxed social environment afterward.

CHAPTER 3

STRENGTH TRAINING FOR BASKETBALL

Basketball is no longer strictly a finesse sport. The profile of today's player bears scant resemblance to the thin and wiry players who graced the courts as little as 10 years ago. From the high school level on up, players must be strong enough to fight through the pick, yet remain nimble enough to spin-dribble through traffic en route to a monster slam dunk.

Players today, therefore, need special strength training to prepare themselves to play their best. The information in this chapter provides a brief overview of strength training. For a more detailed discussion, I recommend two books: *Designing Resistance Training Programs* by Fleck and Kraemer, Human Kinetics and *Weight Training for Life* by James L. Hesson, Morton Publishing.

MISCONCEPTIONS ABOUT STRENGTH TRAINING

There are as many philosophies of strength training as there are iron plates in the weight room. You must realize that, while certain principles remain constant, each program is unique. Just because one particular routine works for one person, doesn't necessarily mean another individual will experience the same degree of success with the identical program. Research has resulted in important insights into the physiological adaptations associated with strength training. As a result, many myths have been dispelled. Unfortunately, misconceptions still abound. Some of the more frequently asked questions include the following.

Won't strength training make me "muscle bound"? Very few people are genetically capable of achieving the massive proportions (hypertrophy) that are the goal of most bodybuilders. Even those who have the "right" genes usually require chemical assistance to grow to the preposterous dimensions we sometimes see. Moreover, bodybuilding requires as much as 6 hours per day—about 6 times the amount of time that a basketball player will spend in the weight room—and a bodybuilder's routine is designed specifically to get "huge." Even though a basketball player may work out at the same gym, training right next to a body-builder and using the same equipment, the final outcome will be dramatically different because of the program's design. The basketball player's primary goal is to become stronger and more powerful, and a strength program can be specifically designed to achieve that end.

Will I lose flexibility by lifting weights? Performed properly through a full range of motion, weight training can actually enhance flexibility.

Will my shot be affected by lifting weights? Shooting a basketball is a fine motor skill, and if you lift weights for an hour, walk onto the floor, and start shooting free throws, more than likely your make percentage will suffer noticeably. Because the muscles "remember" the recent heavy pushing or pulling from the weight room workout, you must now make a conscious effort when shooting the ball. In other words, after years of taking your shot for granted, you now must rehearse correct technique to be successful. Moreover, because of your new-found strength, the range of your shot will increase. So the answer is yes, your shot will be affected, but the effects will be positive.

DESIGNING A PROGRAM

To improve strength levels you must exert force against a resistance that is greater than you normally encounter during daily activities and one that gradually increases. This is the concept of *progressive overload*, which is the basis for strength training programs. At the end of this chapter are several charts to enable you to design a systematic program of progressive overload that is right for you. Before you can use them properly, however, you must understand some basic principles of strength training, including safety considerations; loads, reps, and speed; frequency of lifting; variation in the routine; and general guidelines for establishing a good program.

Safety Considerations

Improper strength training can be dangerous. The first step in designing a program is to carefully study these safety principles:

- Receive medical clearance from your doctor before initiating a strength training program.

- Never train alone. A qualified coach or trainer should be present at all times to help in the event of a mishap and to provide technical assistance.
- Always warm up and stretch prior to strength training. It's a good idea to do one or more warm-up sets before each new lift, especially if the day's program will require heavy weights.
- Make sure the bar is evenly balanced (i.e., equal weight on both sides) and collars are securely fastened.
- Always use correct technique. Never sacrifice form for added weight.
- Remember to breathe. Inhale during the negative segment of the lift. Hold your breath briefly during the initial portion of the positive phase, then gradually exhale through the remainder of the lift.
- Start the session with the primary muscle groups (the larger muscles such as the pecs, lats, quads, hams, etc.) and gradually incorporate auxiliary or smaller musculature (biceps, triceps, forearms, calves, etc.) toward the end of the workout.
- Always use a spotter. Spotting is "as needed" assistance given the lifter at any point or throughout the movement. The spotter should be familiar both with correct technique of the lift being performed and with appropriate spotting procedure, such as initial lift-off, hand placement, and reracking of the weight.
- Young strength trainers (prepubescent) should maintain an 8- to 20-repetitions-per-set regimen. The load they choose should be light enough to accommodate this 8- to 20-repetition set. Avoid overhead lifts.

Reps, Sets, Load, and Speed

A *repetition* is a singular, complete movement. For example, from the locked arm position in the bench press, lowering the weight to the chest, and pressing back to the locked arm position would be one repetition. There will be one or more repetitions per set.

A *set* is a group of repetitions of a particular lift (exercise). The *load* (weight) you choose will be determined by the number of repetitions and sets you plan to perform for each exercise. Let's say that the day's routine calls for 3 sets, the first with 10 reps, the second with 8, and the third with 6 reps. You should select a weight that will challenge you during the last few reps of each set. For example, if you were able to lift

150 pounds for 10 repetitions with ease, the weight was probably too light. If your set called for 10 reps and you were only able to achieve 6, the weight was too heavy. The ideal weight for a set of 10 reps would challenge you so much during reps 8, 9, and 10 that you might require slight assistance from a spotter in order to finish the set. Typically, once you can complete the predetermined repetitions for the set unassisted, the weight would be increased for that lift in the next set, especially if subsequent sets follow a descending repetition pattern (i.e., 10, 8, 6, 4, etc.). This technique of adding weight and lowering the number of repetitions for succeeding sets is called *pyramiding.* **Caution: Young athletes (usually younger than 16) should avoid lifting extremely heavy weights. As a general rule, prepubescent athletes should never do fewer than 8 reps per set.**

When it comes to the speed of the lift, again, there are many differing opinions. Proponents of slow lifting theorize that if the movement is slow, a greater percentage of muscle fibers will be involved in the lift. It is my belief, however, that since basketball is an explosive sport requiring rapid and forceful muscular contractions, training for it should lean toward the explosive. This doesn't mean "throwing" weights around as fast as possible. I advocate a deliberate, yet powerful, contraction of the involved muscles. Let's say a player is performing a bench press. During the negative, or eccentric, portion of the lift (the downward movement when the bar moves from a locked-arm position to the chest), the bar will move more slowly than in the upward (concentric) portion of the lift. Typically, the negative portion should last 1 to 2 seconds, whereas the positive would last less than 1 second. These times are generalizations. Actual speed will be dictated by the type of lift, amount of weight being lifted, fatigue level of the athlete, repetitions, sets, and the length of the rest interval. Slower speeds are less suitable to the explosive nature of basketball, whereas extremely fast lifts can create control problems, which might result in an injury. Never sacrifice technique for speed.

Frequency of Lifting

Resting between training sessions is as important as the actual lifting regimen. In response to the stress of lifting heavy weights, your body builds new muscle tissue, and that muscle build-up occurs during the recovery period. If you lift every day without allowing sufficient rest between sessions, your body lacks adequate time to rebuild muscle and you actually lessen the benefits of your weight training.

In the off-season, the Knicks typically follow a *split routine* 4 days weekly. A split routine emphasizes different body parts in alternating sessions. A typical split session might include chest, shoulders, triceps, and "push" legs on Monday and Thursday; and upper back, lower back, biceps, and "pull" legs on Tuesday and Friday. Another split routine might be upper body one session and lower body the next session. (Auxiliary muscles such as biceps, triceps, forearms, and calves are incorporated regularly into the regimen. Abdominals are performed on a schedule of 3 days on, 1 day off. This means 3 days of abdominal exercises followed by 1 day of rest.) Sufficient recovery occurs using the split routine because there is at least 48 hours of rest between sessions emphasizing the same muscle groups. Even when four or five sessions per week are required, following a split routine will allow for higher intensity (heavier resistance) training that is focused on specific muscle groups.

Novice lifters should follow a 3 day per week *total-body* routine in which all major muscle groups are stressed during each weight training session. Using a Monday, Wednesday, Friday format gives a 24-hour recovery between sessions, which is sufficient rest for achieving significant gains in strength.

Well-organized lifting programs such as the split and total-body routines, can easily be maintained during the off-season. In-season, however, the time and effort spent on practice, games, schoolwork, and jobs may limit your lifting. Strength can be maintained with as little as one **high-intensity** training session weekly, which is far better than no lifting at all. Try to maintain a regular lifting schedule in-season, limiting it as necessary to avoid interfering with other responsibilities.

Although rest is important *between* sessions for maximizing the training effect, rest between sets *during* the session also plays a significant role in strength adaptation. If you rest between sets for 1 to 5 minutes, your body will have much more time to replenish the working muscles with energy. This rest interval is indicative of a *heavy* lifting day. Rest periods of 1 minute or less would be more suitable to developing muscular endurance. Obviously, because of the short rest between sets, fatigue becomes a factor requiring the use of less weight.

Varying the Routine

Programs are organized to maximize to result in strength or conditioning development to peak at a specific time of the training year. Your off-season and pre-season training should be planned so that your maximum strength, speed, power, and conditioning coincide with the start of the season. During the competitive season your training should follow a similar format. Even though duration, frequency, and, to a lesser degree, intensity will be significantly reduced, an in-season program can be designed to allow you to "peak" for the play-offs.

The sample program you will read gives a 6-month (28 week) off-season *macrocycle*. This macrocycle is broken into 4 phases, or *mesocycles*, each lasting 6 weeks. (Note: There is an "Active Rest" period following each 6 week cycle.) These mesocycles are further separated into three easily managed 2-week *microcyles*. Each microcycle will be structured with different numbers of reps, sets, and different *loads*. The goal of each 6-week mesocycle is to have a small "strength peak" that corresponds with the end of one mesocycle and the beginning of the next. The combination of all the mesocycle peaks will culminate in a large "strength peak" at the end of the off-season macrocyle and the start of the regular season.

Each of the four mesocycles within the macrocycle features a different primary focus. During the first part of the off-season (mesocycles 1 and 2) the emphasis is on developing a solid base of strength and conditioning. In the later stages of the off- and pre-season (mesocycles 3 and 4) the emphasis is on strength and power development. The reps, sets, and load will be reflective of this plan.

Similarly, each microcycle within a mesocycle is distinct. The first 2-week microcycle focuses on muscular endurance. The last 2 weeks of the cycle accentuate muscular strength, and the middle 2 weeks are a combination of the two. Each new microcycle features progressively greater loads. As the competitive season approaches, emphasis shifts from loads of lighter weight with more reps (muscular endurance) to loads of heavier weight with fewer reps (muscular strength and power). During the latter stage of the preparation phase (off-season macrocycle), the focus shifts from conditioning to more specific technique work. As a general rule, to determine whether muscular strength or muscular endurance is being emphasized, remember that less than 8 reps per set would be indicative of muscular strength while 12 or more per set would enhance muscular endurance.

Guidelines for Designing a Strength Training Program

1. *Load* is based on the number of reps to be performed. Use the heaviest weight you can while remaining able to complete the pre-scribed repetitions per set. Remember, never sacrifice technique for added poundage.

2. While the anatomical focus will remain constant, the actual lifts car vary from day to day. For example, on Monday you may perform a la

pull behind the head; Wednesday, lat pull to the chest; Friday, lat pullover on a flat bench, and so on. This same principle can be applied to every body part. Keep good records so that when you come back to a lift down the road, you'll know at what intensity you have been working.

3. When the training focus is either *muscular endurance, muscular endurance/strength,* or *muscular strength,* the volume of **total** sets per session should not exceed 30. In other words,

$$\text{Total \# of lifts} \times \text{Total sets per lift} < \text{or} = 30$$

For example, on Monday you may do 5 sets for each of 2 lifts for the upper back, 3 sets of 2 lifts for the lower back and legs, and 3 sets for each of 1 lift for the shoulders and chest. Total *lifts* for this particular workout would be 8. Total *sets* would therefore be 28 (see below).

Anatomical focus	Total # of lifts	Total sets per lift	Total sets per musculature
Upper back	2	5	10
Lower back	2	3	6
Shoulders	1	3	3
Chest	1	3	3
Legs	2	3	6
		Total sets per workout	28

Then on Wednesday you could try 3 sets of each of 2 lifts for each anatomical focus, resulting in 30 total sets for the workout. Friday, you might do 3 sets of only 1 lift each for the upper back, lower back, and shoulders but 5 sets of 2 lifts for the chest and legs. This routine would result in a total sets per workout of 29.

4. Toward the end of the macrocycle when the training focus shifts to *muscular strength/power* and / or *muscular power,* the total volume of sets will drop to 24 or less. This will allow for increased intensity and longer rest intervals between sets while maintaining a reasonable duration of the lifting session. **Note: Because of the increased intensity, young athletes (approximately age 16 or less) should not advance to the muscular strength/power, and/or muscular power training focus.**

5. When performing only 1 exercise per anatomical focus, select a multi-joint lift (referred to as a *compound lift*). The majority of lifts for all

regions of the body (with the exception of the lower back musculature) are compound. Examine the lift and determine if more than one joint will be involved in the movement. For example, compound lifts for the legs that involve the hip, knee, and ankle joints would include the squat, leg press, and various lunges.

6. While I do not consider auxiliary muscles when determining total volume of sets, these muscles should certainly not be ignored. Time and energy usually dictate load, sets, and reps for these muscles.

7. Total volume does not include the warm-up set.

LIFT OPTIONS FOR MUSCLE GROUPS

Anatomical focus	Primary muscle groups	Lift options
Back	Latissimus dorsi—"lat" Middle and lower trapezius — "trap" Rhomboid Spinal erector (sacrospinalis)	Lat pull—various hand grip positions Lat pullover Chin-ups Seated bentover row Seated pulley row Dumbbell bent knee deadlift Prone hyperextension
Shoulders	Upper "trap" Levator scapulae Deltoid group	Shoulder press Upright row Lateral deltoid raise Front deltoid raise Rear deltoid raise Shrug
Chest	Pectoralis major Anterior deltoid Pectoralis minor	Bench press Incline press Push-ups Dumbbell flys—flat or incline bench Cable crossover flys Dips
Legs—front	Quadriceps group -Vastus lateralis -Vastus intermedius -Vastus medialis -Rectus femoris Adductor group Abductor group	Knee extension
Legs—back	Hamstring group -Biceps femoris -Semitendinosus Gluteus group	Knee curl
Legs— compound		Leg press Squats Lunges—forward, 45 degree, and lateral Step-ups

Anatomical focus	Auxiliary muscle groups	Lift options
Arms	Biceps Triceps Forearm group	Biceps curl—variations Triceps pushdown Triceps dumbbell kickbacks
Calves	Gastrocnemius Soleus	Straight leg calf raise Seated calf raise

OFF-SEASON MACROCYCLE—28 WEEKS

Design every set to include 1-4 lifts for each of the four anatomical focus areas listed in "Lift Options for Muscle Groups" (see p. 52). Each lift should be performed for the same range of reps within a given set. Remember that lifts for the auxiliary muscle groups (arms and calves) should be performed daily as time allows.

Mesocycle I—6 Weeks
Seasonal phase: early off-season
Primary training focus: muscular endurance

	Microcycle 1 (2 weeks)	Microcycle 2 (2 weeks)	Microcycle 3 (2 weeks)
Focus:	Endurance	Endurance/strength	Strength
Load:	Light	Light to moderate	Moderate to heavy
Rest:	< 1 minute	1-2 minutes	> 2 minutes
Sets:	3-5	3-5	3-5
Reps/lift:	12-15	10-12	Week 1: 8
			Week 2: 6-8

Active Rest—1 Week

Total body circuit training: high intensity, 2-3 sets/8-10 reps, 2-3 days/week

Mesocycle II—6 Weeks
Seasonal phase: early to mid off-season
Primary training focus: muscular endurance/strength

	Microcycle 1 (2 weeks)	Microcycle 2 (2 weeks)	Microcycle 3 (2 weeks)
Focus:	Endurance	Endurance/strength	Strength
Load:	Light	Light to moderate	Moderate to heavy
Rest:	< 1 minute	1-2 minutes	> 2 minutes
Sets:	3-5	3-5	3-5
Reps/lift:	12	Week 1: 10-12	Week 1: 8
		Week 2: 8-10	Week 2: 6-8

Active Rest—1 Week

Total body circuit training: high intensity, 2-3 sets/8-10 reps, 2-3 days/week

Mesocycle III—6 Weeks

Seasonal phase: mid off-season to pre-season
Primary training focus: muscular strength

	Microcycle 1 (2 weeks)	Microcycle 2 (2 weeks)	Microcycle 3 (2 weeks)
Focus:	Endurance/strength	Strength	Strength/power
Load:	Light to moderate	Moderate to heavy	Heavy
Rest:	1-2 minutes	> 2 minutes	> 3 minutes
Sets:	3-5	3-5	Week 1: 3-5
			Week 2: 3-6
Reps/lift:	Modified pyramid (12,10,8, optional 8,8)	6-8	Week 1: 4-6 Week 2: Pyramid each lift (8,6,5,4 ...)

Active Rest—1 Week

Total body circuit training: high intensity, 2-3 sets/8-10 reps, 2-3 days/week

Mesocycle IV—6 Weeks

Seasonal phase: pre-season
Primary training focus: muscular strength/power

	Microcycle 1 (2 weeks)	Microcycle 2 (2 weeks)	Microcycle 3 (2 weeks)
Focus:	Strength	Strength/power	Power
Load:	Moderate to heavy	Heavy	Very heavy
Rest:	> 2 minutes	> 3 minutes	> 4 minutes
Sets:	3-5	3-5	Week 1: 5
			Week 2: 5
Reps/lift:	6-8	Week 1: 4-6 Week 2: Pyramid each lift (8,6,5,4...)	Week 1: Pyramid each lift (8,6,4,3,2) Week 2: Pyramid each lift (8,6,4,3,2)

Active Rest—1 Week

Total body circuit training: high intensity, 2-3 sets/8-10 reps, 2-3 days/week

SAMPLE WEEKLY STRENGTH TRAINING ROUTINE

Mesocycle IV
Microcycle II   *Ideal for varsity athletes. Not recommended for prepubescent*
Week 1   *athletes.*
Training focus: Muscular strength/power
Load (intensity):   Heavy
Rest interval/set: > 3 minutes
Total sets/session: < 24

*Indicates warm-up set(s) and is not included in total sets per session.
Note: An exception is made for some muscle groups (i.e., deltoid musculature) or if training isolaterally (i.e., lunges) regarding number of sets per lift.

Monday—back emphasis

Anatomical focus	Lift	Sets and reps
Back	Lat pull—behind the head	10*, 4,4,4
	Seated pulley row	6,5,4
	Dumbbell bent knee deadlift	6,6
Chest	Flat bench press	10*,8*,6,5,4,4,4
Shoulders	Upright row	10*,6,6,6
	Shrug	6,6,6
Legs	Leg press	<u>15*,10*,6,6,6,6</u>
	Total sets per session	**23**

Wednesday—chest and shoulder emphasis

Anatomical focus	Lift	Sets and reps
Chest	Incline bench press	10*,6,5,4
	Dumbbell flys—flat bench	5,5,5
	Dips	2 sets to failure
Back	Dumbbell seated bentover row	10*,6,5,4
	Chin-ups—reverse close grip	5,5
Shoulders	Lateral deltoid raise	5,5
	Front deltoid raise	5,5
	Rear deltoid raise	5,5
Legs	Squats	10*,6,6,6
	Lunges—45 degree	<u>6,6 each leg</u>
	Total sets per session	**24**

Friday—leg emphasis

Anatomical focus	Lift	Sets and reps
Legs	Squats	10*,8*,6,5,4
	Knee extension	6,6,6
	Knee curl	6,6,6
	Lunges—forward	6,6 each leg
Back	Lat pull—to the chest	6,6,6
	Lat pullover	6,6,6
Chest	Dumbbell incline bench press	8*,6,5,4
Shoulders	Shoulder press	6,5,4
	Total sets per session	**23**

CHAPTER 4

ABDOMINAL AND LOWER BACK STRENGTH

An often overlooked and undertrained part of the body's musculature is the trunk and low torso. Referred to as the "center of power," this region of the body is either directly responsible for the origin of a movement, or is the stabilization link through which all movements pass.

Here are some good reasons why you should strengthen your abdominals and lower back:

- The muscles controlling the trunk and low torso are essential for the maintenance of the body's balance, agility, and coordination when performing movement tasks.
- 50% of the body's total mass is located within this region.
- Low back pain and injury often disrupt training and result in missed games. Strengthening the trunk and low torso effectively decreases the incidence and/or severity of low back injuries.

Following are guidelines for training the "center of power." This basic abdominal strengthening routine should be incorporated into your training regimen.

GUIDELINES FOR ABDOMINAL TRAINING

- *Start with one set of four to six repetitions for each exercise.* As your strength levels improve, increase the number of repetitions per set, and gradually increase the number of sets per session. Sets and repetitions will vary depending on the training phase (e.g., off-season, pre-season, in-season). Never sacrifice form for added sets and reps.

- *Try to maintain a tight abdominal contraction throughout the set.* Keep rest to a minimum between sets and never rest between exercises during a set.

- *Always fatigue the "weaker" muscles first.* Therefore, to maximize abdominal strength development, follow this sequence: (1) oblique; (2) lower abdominal; and (3) upper abdominal. Because the upper abdominal assists with movements in the oblique and lower abdominal region, it's important not to fatigue the upper abdominal musculature first, which would decrease the amount of work performed by the other muscles of the trunk and low torso.

- *Avoid exercises that place the spine in an arched position, such as straight-leg sit-ups, leg raises, and so on* (see figures below).

- *Keep workouts balanced.* Always train opposing muscle groups equally to prevent muscle imbalances. For example, after an abdominal workout, do several sets of low back extensions.

STRAIGHT LEG OBLIQUE CRUNCH

Focus: Oblique musculature

Procedure: Lie on the left side, legs straight. Put the right hand behind the head, and the left hand lightly touching the working oblique muscles. "Crunch" the right oblique musculature. Avoid an excessive backward lean. The movement is directly to the side.

Duration: Hold for a two count in the up position. Perform one complete set and repeat on the opposite side.

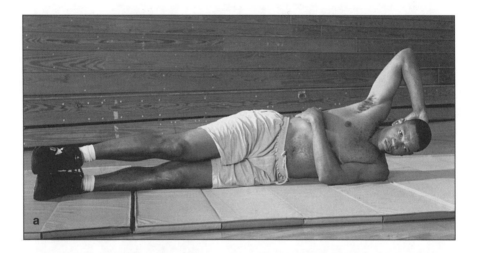

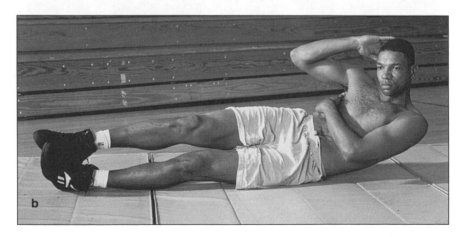

BENT KNEE OBLIQUE TWIST

Focus: Oblique and upper abdominal musculature

Procedure: Lie with the shoulders flat to the floor, knees bent and twisted to the left side. Place both hands behind the head (do not pull on the head or neck during any abdominal exercise). "Crunch" the abdominal musculature and hold the up position for a two count. *Note:* Focus on the muscles being trained. Avoid rolling the shoulders; rather, lift the head and shoulders toward the ceiling (keep the head back slightly).

Duration: Perform one complete set and repeat on the opposite side.

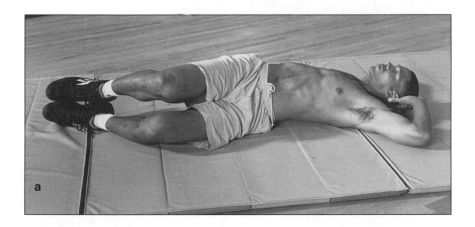

LOW "AB" CRUNCH

Focus: Low abdominal musculature

Procedure: Lying supine, knees and hips are flexed to a 90° angle. Hands are across the chest or positioned lightly behind the head. "Crunch" the low abdomen only and lift the hips approximately 3 to 6 inches up and back. Don't rock back, because rocking allows momentum to assist in the movement. Slowly lower the hips and lower body down to the floor and immediately repeat.

Duration: Continue until all repetitions in the set have been completed.

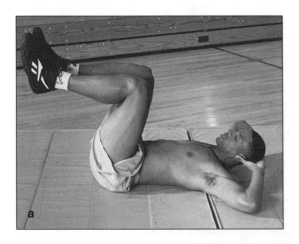

CROSS-OVERS

Focus: Upper abdominal and oblique musculature

Procedure: Cross the right leg over the left leg. The left foot is flat on the floor. Hands are either across the chest or positioned lightly behind the head (do not pull on the head and neck). Contract the abdominal musculature, lift, twist, then touch the left elbow to the right knee. Hold for a two count. Slowly return the shoulder blades to the floor, tap, and immediately repeat.

Duration: Perform one complete set and repeat with the left leg over the right.

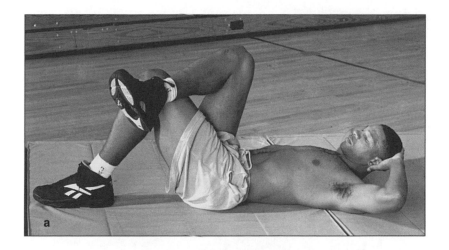

CURL-UPS

Focus: Upper abdominal musculature

Procedure: Lie supine with the soles of the feet together, knees flared to the sides. The position of the arms determines the difficulty of the drill: (a) Easiest—extend arms between the legs. (b) Moderately difficult—fold arms across the chest. (c) Most difficult—position hands behind the head. Contract the upper abdominal musculature. Shoulder blades will raise only about 6 to 8 inches off the floor. Hold for a two count. Slowly lower the upper body to the floor, tap the shoulder blades, and immediately repeat.

Duration: Continue until all repetitions in the set have been completed.

Variation: To involve the oblique musculature, try a "lift and twist." Make sure to train both sides.

WRIST-UPS

Focus: Upper abdominal musculature

Procedure: Lie supine with feet flat on the floor. Place hands on the thighs with finger tips pointed toward the knee. Count two going up, hold for two counts in the up position, and count two going down. In the up position the wrists should crest the knees (no higher). Keep the chin tucked in when down, and back when in the up position. Do not allow the abdominal muscles to relax at any time during this exercise.

Duration: Continue until all repetitions in the set have been completed.

90 DEGREE CRUNCH

Focus: Upper abdominal musculature

Procedure: Lie supine, with knees and hips flexed at a 90° angle. Use the same arm position used for Curl-Ups. "Crunch" the upper abdominal musculature and lift the shoulders off the floor. Touch the elbows to the knees and hold for a two count. Maintain hip and knee flexion at 90° throughout the exercise.

Duration: Continue until all repetitions in the set have been completed.

SKYWALKERS

Focus: Upper abdominal musculature

Procedure: Lie supine, flexing hips at a 90° angle, and fully extending the knees. Keep the arms straight and hands together. "Crunch" the upper abdominal musculature and reach to the feet. Touch the left foot, tap the floor with the shoulder blades, immediately touch the right foot.

Duration: Continue until all repetitions in the set have been completed.

LOW BACK HYPEREXTENSIONS

Focus: Low back musculature

Procedure: Lie in a prone position with legs straight and arms extended overhead. Slowly raise both the legs and arms up from the floor (knees and elbows should be only 2 to 3 inches off the floor). Hold for about 5 seconds, slowly lower back to the floor and repeat.

Duration: Perform 10 to 15 repetitions per set.

Variations: Some variations from the same position include lifting the

- upper body and arms only,
- legs only,
- right arm/left leg, then switch, and
- left arm/left leg, then switch.

If you perform these exercises regularly, you'll see and feel the development of your trunk and lower torso. A strong "center of power" will benefit you in strengthening other parts of the body for basketball-specific purposes.

CHAPTER 5

ATHLETICISM FOR BASKETBALL

The physical requirements necessary to play basketball at a highly competitive level are far beyond those needed to perform common daily activities, and even surpass the demands of most other sports. Basic fitness alone isn't going to cut it. Good flexibility (chapter 2), strength (chapter 3), and abdominal and low back strength (chapter 4) are three essentials I've already noted. But even these are not enough. You must also develop attributes associated with heightened athletic performance. This chapter, while not exhaustive, stresses a number of other athletic skills needed to be a superior basketball player:

- Speed
- Power
- Agility
- Coordination

All four of these athletic abilities are partially genetically determined. Some players are "wired" a bit better than others. They are what the uninformed basketball broadcaster would call a *natural athlete*.

But heredity plays a smaller role than most people think. Far too many genetically gifted players have let that ability go to waste, whereas other players have pushed themselves to the limits of their athletic potential. In other words, if you want to improve your speed, power, agility, and coordination you can.

In this chapter I provide the information and conditioning exercises you need to become a better athlete. But don't put the cart before the horse. Make sure you first establish a solid fitness base using the first four chapters. Only then should you try to raise your athleticism to new heights.

SPEED

Speed, quickness, and jumping ability are the athletic skills often considered most valuable for basketball. Players who look smooth, effortless, and explosive on the court compared to their opponents are the ones who generally excel in the sport. They have developed superior fundamental movement skills that allow them to get from point A to point B very quickly. This distance may be one step, from the floor to the rim, from baseline to baseline, and so on.

Speed has two basic components: *stride length* (the amount of distance covered in a single step), and *stride frequency* (the number of steps taken per unit of time). The cadence at which the athlete moves his or her arms and legs, and the distance each stride covers, determines an athlete's speed. Ideally, a player will achieve a high rate of frequency to accompany a long stride. This also holds true for movements other than straight-ahead sprinting such as lateral, backward, and combination movements.

All players have inherent limitations as to how fast they can move their arms and legs. In fact, world class sprinters and average weekend warriors are surprisingly similar in terms of stride frequency. Granted, almost every athlete could stand to improve the frequency of his or her stride. But, from a time management perspective, more progress in speed development is made by emphasizing the development of an "explosive" stride, like Kevin Johnson's or Sheryl Swoopes'. Just make sure you don't sacrifice stride frequency for added stride length.

If the greatest limiting factor to developing speed is stride length, then why can't the athlete just run with a longer stride? The answer is that what the athlete gains in stride length is usually offset by a loss of movement efficiency. Anyone can go out and run with a longer stride, but overstriding, extraneous movements (twisting, bobbing, etc.), and reduced stride frequency almost always produce a longer stride at the expense of total speed.

The three keys to improving stride length are to

1. increase muscular power,
2. improve flexibility in the body joints involved in the movement, and
3. improve the mechanics of the movement.

A player won't develop speed merely by practicing fast movements.

Fundamental movement patterns such as running, hopping, skipping, jumping, shuffling, and back-pedaling are common in the game of basketball. Now that you know the importance of specificity (chapter 1) and want to develop a more efficient and longer stride, you'll want to include a program of drills and activities for improving speed and quickness in your training regimen. Several of these fundamental movement patterns are described and illustrated at the end of the chapter. And because these movements can be incorporated into the court drills presented in chapters 8 and 9, you can improve your basketball-specific movement patterns and enhance the appropriate energy system at the same time.

POWER

Of critical importance to successful athletic performance is the ability to generate power. In basketball, when all other attributes between two players are about equal, the more powerful athlete will usually win.

The formula for determining power is:

$$\text{Power} = \text{Force} \times \text{Distance}/\text{Time}.$$

What this formula means in simple terms is that to become a more powerful basketball player you need to exert maximal force in the shortest amount of time.

Recall that strength is defined as the maximum amount of force a muscle can generate. So strength plays a vital role in the power equation. Yet, coaches and players still make the mistake of confusing strength with power and therefore mistakenly judge power by how much weight a player can lift in the weight room. This isn't a measure of power but rather an indicator of absolute strength, and is of little value if it isn't readily transferable to the basketball floor.

Conversely, a powerful athlete is able to incorporate maximum force with speed of movement. Explosive power is also called *dynamic* or *functional strength* and should be the goal of any resistance training program.

Plyometric training is an extremely effective way of combining speed with strength, resulting in dynamic strength (power). Jumping, hopping, skipping, bounding, medicine ball chest passes, and abdominal twist tosses are just a few of the hundreds of plyometric exercises that can enhance the speed component of power.

The physiological adaptations associated with plyometric training are neuromuscular in nature. Plyometrics utilize the natural elastic tendencies of the muscle and the reflex potentiation to generate greater force production. One might think of the principles of plyometrics as that of stretching a rubber band and then releasing it. As the rubber band is stretched, energy is stored in the elastic properties of the rubber. As tension is released, the energy is released in an equal and opposite reaction. Plyometrics facilitate the *loading* of a muscle or group of muscles, inducing a rapid *stretch* that elicits a neural response resulting in a more forceful reactive contraction.

Three Keys to Becoming a More Powerful Player

The process of developing power for basketball should be focused on the development of improved speed, strength, and mechanics.

- **Improved Speed**

To improve overall movement skills (e.g., forward, backward, lateral, and combinations), your focus should be on developing a powerful stride length while maintaining a quick stride frequency. This will allow you to cover more ground while maintaining the proverbial "quick feet" that coaches typically view as an important characteristic of effective basketball players. Power is the ability to exert explosive force, which might be generated by the chest, shoulders, and triceps when executing a chest pass, or the timely contraction of the muscles that extend the ankles, knees, hips, and shoulders just prior to a vertical jump. The speed with which the muscles involved are able to contract and apply force determines the power output. In other words, the faster the application of force, the greater the potential for increased power.

Another factor is the absolute amount of mass or weight that must be moved. If you're carrying excessive weight in the form of extra body fat, it would be to your benefit to develop a realistic fat loss program coupled with a strength training regimen to increase your strength and ultimately enhance lean muscle tissue. With less fat and more muscle, you'll have the potential to move more explosively.

- **Improved Strength**

The ability to exert force explosively—to move powerfully—requires adequate amounts of muscular strength. Therefore, the greater the strength of the athlete, the greater the potential for increased force production.

Strength is valuable to a basketball player only if it's readily transferable to the basketball court. It's difficult to replicate in the weight room, with any accuracy, the many movement patterns that you'll execute during a practice or game situation. Functional strength training attempts to link the weight room to the playing floor.

The use of medicine balls, running harnesses, weighted vests, and step and hill running are just a few of the alternative methods of overloading the system in an attempt to build strength and power specifically for basketball action (see Figures a, b, c, and d). Movement patterns used on the court, such as back-pedaling, sprinting, and lateral shuffling, can all be enhanced by overloading these movements through the practice of functional strength training principles incorporated into your training regimen.

- **Improved Mechanics**

Using the most efficient movements to successfully perform a skill is essential for the realization of more power. Combine speed and strength with the correct mechanics and your power production will make appreciable gains. The fundamental movement patterns detailed at the end of this chapter are designed to help you learn correct form and efficient movement.

Range of Motion

One way to move more freely and with greater speed and agility is to develop good flexibility. In addition, the ability to perform without fear of injury will result in more powerful actions. With a rubber band, the magnitude of the stretch dictates the amount of stored energy and consequent energy release. With muscle, it's not the magnitude, but rather the speed of the stretch that ultimately determines power generation.

But every so often a muscle is stretched to its limits. Being able to withstand the rigors of a maximal stretch and still execute a powerful move and not injure yourself is extremely important for long-term durability and productivity. Range of motion (flexibility) is an important factor in becoming a total athlete.

AGILITY

Closely aligned with balance, *agility* requires athletes to regulate shifts in the body's center of gravity while subjecting themselves to postural deviations. Agility is the ability to change direction without decreasing speed.

For example, Anthony Mason of the Knicks has the uncanny ability to sprint the length of the floor and, in two "gather" steps, immediately change direction. Imagine a man 6'7" tall, 255 pounds, who can bench press 400 pounds and leg press 1,100 pounds, sprinting full speed, then, 5 feet in front of you, suddenly blasting to your left or right seeming to have never slowed down a step. Most players must decelerate considerably in order to gain control prior to a quick change of direction.

Minimizing the amount of deceleration is a key factor in improving agility. The ability to change direction rapidly explains to a large degree why high jumpers can leap so high. The high jumper establishes his or her speed during the approach and then transfers this horizontal speed to vertical lift in the last two quick steps prior to the take-off. These same characteristics can be incorporated into movements on the basketball court.

You should include drills that require rapid changes of direction in your daily training regimen. With frequent practice at switching quickly from forward, backward, lateral, and vertical movements, you'll improve your agility. Use the many agility drills presented later in this book, or make up your own. Just get moving!

COORDINATION

Often thought of as synonymous with agility, *coordination* is the ability to organize all the components of fitness and attributes of athleticism into sync. Coordination involves the concept of synergy. *Synergy* means that the *whole* product is greater than the sum of its *parts*. This concept gave rise to the whole-part-whole teaching method of sports skills.

For example, let's say that an athlete wanted to learn how to juggle three balls (an outstanding hand/eye coordination activity). Without prior instruction the athlete probably wouldn't be too successful by just tossing all three balls simultaneously into the air. Instead, you'd show the athlete how the skill is performed with a brief demonstration. Next you'd teach the athlete the single ball toss, followed by the double ball pattern once the single ball toss was mastered. This progression would continue until the athlete was juggling three balls.

So, when learning a movement or activity, and adhering to the concept of synergy, you should

1. see or demonstrate the *whole* movement;

2. break down the movement into its *parts*;

3. master each *part* of the *whole* movement; and

4. reassemble the *parts* to create an improved *whole* movement.

Practicing coordination allows for the harmonious integration of all movements in a smooth, controlled, and efficient action. By practicing each movement, or—better yet—each part of each movement, the athlete will greatly enhance the total effort.

All of this is to say that **agility and coordination can be learned**. An athlete can effectively improve performance and decrease the risk of injury by simply improving his or her agility and coordination. Most of the movements presented in the following section and in the court drills provided later in the book demand a moderate-to-high degree of coordination. Yet, even if you're lacking some agility and coordination, you too will benefit from working at these activities until you can complete most of them successfully.

FUNDAMENTAL MOVEMENT PATTERNS

The next time you're watching a game, look beyond the behind-the-back passes, slam dunks, and three pointers, and make an effort to track *one* player's movements. Better yet, watch a game on film, in slow motion, and notice how a player gets from point A to point B. If you look closely you will see *fundamental movements* such as hopping, jumping, skipping, bounding, running, and galloping in forward, backward, lateral, and vertical directions.

Fundamental movement patterns are developmental skills that children learn, and serve as foundational movements for more advanced sport-specific skills. The ability to move explosively and efficiently is critical to successful basketball performance. Natural athletes execute these fundamental movement patterns with a high degree of proficiency. Such players are remarkably explosive, yet their movements on court look smooth and effortless.

For the most part, the court drills outlined in chapters 8 and 9 require sprinting, lateral power shuffling (step slide), back or defensive shuffling, back-pedaling, and a variety of jumps. Movements that may be substituted for these include high-knee running, heel kicks, skipping, carioca, and back sprinting.

Include a variety of these movement patterns when using the drills with which you choose to train. By continually altering the routine, you challenge your athletic ability to adapt to a constantly changing physical stress. If you decide to use some of the drills for assessment purposes, then you must use the same movement patterns from one test to the next.

Following are brief descriptions and illustrations of the basic and optional fundamental movement patterns that I encourage you to incorporate into your training. If you are having difficulty mastering the technique, remember the whole-part-whole concept. Closely examine the whole movement pattern. Break the whole movement into its parts and practice each part. Then reassemble the parts. Don't give up.

Basic Movement Patterns

The following movement patterns are basic to the development of more advanced basketball-specific movement skills.

SPRINTING

- Notice the straight body alignment with shoulder, hip, knee, and ankle all in a straight line during the push phase.
- The head is up and eyes focused ahead.
- The shoulders are relaxed, and arm action is from the shoulder. Hands come to chin level on the front swing, elbows stop at shoulder level on the back swing. The elbow is at 90° as the hand passes the hip. There is no twisting of the upper body.
- The leg is fully extended as it pushes off the ground, followed by a heel recovery, where the heel nearly grazes the buttocks before the hip joint flexes for an explosive knee drive. The thigh is parallel to the ground during the knee drive phase.

POWER SHUFFLE (STEP SLIDE)

- Keep the head up, back straight, knees flexed, and arms in a defensive ready position. Don't lean forward at the waist.
- Flex the knees to insure a low center of gravity.
- If moving to the left, turn the left foot slightly toward the direction of travel and keep the right foot perpendicular to the direction of travel. Simultaneously push off the right leg while forcefully driving the left knee in the direction of travel. Once the left foot makes contact with the ground, pull with the left leg and slide the right foot to the left (don't cross the right foot in front of the left).

BACK SHUFFLE OR DEFENSIVE SLIDE

- Keep the head up, back straight, knees flexed, and arms in a defensive ready position. Don't lean forward at the waist.
- Maintain a low center of gravity through knee and hip flexion.
- The head, trunk, and torso should face opposite the direction of travel, and the lead foot (Doc's left foot) should be perpendicular to the direction of travel. The trailing foot (Doc's right foot) should point opposite the direction of travel.
- Push off with the trailing foot and immediately pull with the lead foot. The trailing foot should slide too, but should not cross in front of the lead foot.
- Avoid bobbing up and down during the movement. There should be no extraneous movement of the upper torso and head.

BACK-PEDAL

- "Nose over the toes," with a slight forward lean of the upper body.
- Keep the head up and back straight.
- The shoulders should be relaxed. Quick arm action at the shoulder through an abbreviated range of motion.
- Stay on the balls of the feet, using a short, quick stride. Increase speed only when comfortable with the technique.

Additional Movement Patterns

To further enhance your movement skills, you can use the following movement patterns in addition to, or as substitutes for, the basic ones previously described.

HIGH-KNEE RUNNING

- Use this drill as a *part* method for teaching or learning the fundamental movement pattern of sprinting.
- Keep the body alignment straight (that is, keep the shoulder, hip, knee, and ankle in a straight line during the push phase).
- The head is up and eyes focused ahead.
- The shoulders are relaxed and arm action is from the shoulder. Unlike sprinting, the arm action for high-knee running is abbreviated.
- The knee lift is exaggerated as the thigh goes above parallel to the ground.
- Keep stride length short (approximately 2- to 3-foot strides) and tempo fast.
- Stay on the balls of the feet. Be quick off the ground.

HEEL KICKS (THE RECOVERY PHASE OF THE SPRINT ACTION)

- Use this drill as a part method for teaching or learning the fundamental movement pattern of sprinting.
- After the foot leaves the ground, bend the knee sharply. The degree of flexibility of the quadriceps musculature will dictate the range of motion at the knee.
- Ideally, touch the buttocks with the heels (attempt this only if free of knee problems).
- Don't lift the knee. Point the knee straight to the ground throughout the drill.
- Keep the tempo fast but controlled.
- Stay on the balls of the feet. Be quick off the ground.

POWER SKIPS

- Keep the body alignment straight (that is, keep the shoulder, hip, knee, and ankle in a straight line during the push phase).
- The head is up and eyes focused ahead.
- The shoulders are relaxed and arm action is from the shoulder. Exaggerate the arm action, stopping arms at chin level on the front swing, and stopping elbows at shoulder height on the back swing. There is no twisting of the upper body.
- Keep the upper thigh of the driving knee above a position parallel to the ground, maximum hip flexion (see Figure a).
- Cover as much ground as possible during the "flight" phase.
- Make a quick transition during the skip (i.e., right leg to left and vice versa; see Figure b).

CARIOCA

- Keep the head up, back straight, and arms in the defensive ready position (the arms will assist during the movement).
- The upper body is facing 90° to the direction of travel throughout the drill.
- Point the left foot slightly in the direction of travel. (Assume movement is to the left.)
- Step to the side with the left foot (see Figure a).
- Step behind the left foot with the right foot.
- Step to the side again with the left foot.
- Simultaneously turn the hips toward the direction of travel and forcefully drive the right leg (upper thigh above parallel to the ground) across and in front of the left leg (see Figure b). There should be a significant "flight" phase during this portion of the movement. Cover as much ground as possible on the "cross-in-front" step.

BACK SPRINT

- Keep the head up and back straight. Arms swing from the shoulder through a full range of motion, with no twisting of the upper body.
- Lean forward slightly at the waist, but run tall.
- Maintain a good cyclic action of the hip, knee, and ankle.
- The knee lift is approximately 45° just before reach back.
- Extend fully at the hip to allow for an exaggerated stride length.
- When the foot of the extended leg makes contact with the ground, ride the momentum and give a forceful push as the upper body passes over the ground leg.

CHAPTER 6

TESTING BASKETBALL FITNESS

Aerobic and anaerobic conditioning, muscular strength and endurance, flexibility, speed, power, and agility are important fitness and athletic factors associated with basketball performance. In this chapter you'll find a variety of tests to help you gauge your current status. Testing allows you to judge the effectiveness of a training program. Is it producing the gains you sought when starting the program? Tests also help determine the degree of detraining after inactivity, and identify your strengths and weaknesses, indicating what to focus on in your training.

Based on the results of periodic testing, you can set or adjust your conditioning goals. Depending on your scores, you might wish to emphasize training the anaerobic energy system; to add muscle to your game with a progressive strength training program; or to refine your movement skills to become quicker and more agile on the court.

Although a coach can help, the individual goals you pursue should be ones that *you* select, the ones that you are willing to commit to. It's extremely important to establish sensible, attainable, short-term training goals. These types of goals encourage frequent self-assessment and program evaluation. They also provide more positive reinforcement than do long-term goals.

Whatever your goals, continually monitor your progress with testing and adjust your training accordingly. Keep detailed training records in a daily journal or log. These records should be based on measurable results, which will then be used to structure and modify subsequent workouts. People who don't keep records typically train at a level below their physiological capacity, experience limited physical gains, rarely achieve their selected standards, and become very sporadic and do not adhere to a regular training program.

When used correctly, testing can be a motivational tool and help develop realistic goals and maintain a solid work ethic.

TESTING SCHEDULE

For most players, two to four tests a year on each major variable is appropriate. I recommend three testing sessions per year:

1. *End of the off-season.* This is the testing period every lazy person fears. Scores will indicate the effectiveness of the off-season conditioning program.

2. *Midway through the regular season.* Scores obtained at this time help guard against a detraining effect. Some coaches and players decrease the volume of their conditioning too much in favor of greater emphasis on technical skill development during the season.

3. *End of the season.* These test scores will be used to design the off-season training regimen, to establish a baseline to judge the effectiveness of that regimen, and to develop realistic goals.

FIELD TESTS

While it's important to know your general health and fitness status, the following field tests are designed to determine your physical pluses and minuses as a basketball player. These tests require minimal equipment and can be done quickly.

20-YARD DASH

Purpose: Basketball coaches often praise athletes who demonstrate superior speed and quickness. When defining speed, one must differentiate between speed of reaction and speed of movement. Reaction time is the interval of time that separates the presentation of a stimulus (i.e., "Get set! Go!") and the initiation of a movement. Speed of movement is the rate at which you move your body from one location to another. The time required to perform both of these variables (speed of reaction and speed of movement) is response time. The 20-yard dash is an excellent measure of absolute response time.

Procedure:

1. In an unobstructed and level area, measure off 20 yards and place a strip of athletic tape at the start and finish line. Be sure there is an adequate deceleration area beyond the finish line.

2. The tester should stand at the finish line with stopwatch in hand and arm raised. The tester will drop his or her arm on the command "Get set! Go!" The "Go" part of the command should coincide with the arm contacting the tester's leg and the start of the stopwatch.

3. The athlete reacts to the "Go" command and sprints **past** the finish line. The watch will be stopped as the torso crosses the finish line.

4. Record the best time from three trials.

STANDING REACH

Purpose: To determine the athlete's absolute reach.

Procedure: This test can be performed using a single-arm reach. However, it's been my experience that the single-arm reach does not provide very good data on subsequent trials. In an effort to improve the accuracy and reliability of this measure, I use a double-arm reach protocol. Choose between these two methods, but use one method consistently so that you can accurately compare results to previous and subsequent tests.

Procedure Using a Vertec:

1. Take a position directly under the extended flags.

2. Keep the feet together and flat on the floor.

3. Extend both arms with hands next to one another, index fingers touching.

4. Take a deep breath, fully extend the body, and reach up and push away all the flags that can be reached.

5. Make two attempts and record the highest flag moved.

Procedure Using a Wall:

1. Stand facing a wall with the toes touching the wall.
2. Keep the feet together and flat on the floor.
3. Extend both arms with hands next to one another, index fingers touching.
4. Take a deep breath and reach.
5. Mark the highest point reached.
6. Extend a yardstick up from the highest point reached. Attach the yardstick to the wall.

VERTICAL JUMP (NO STEP)

Purpose: To determine power or the application of great force in a very brief time. Often the strongest basketball player is not necessarily the most powerful athlete. Because power is a relationship between strength and speed of movement, tests for strength and tests for power should not be confused. One of the best methods to accurately assess explosive power in the legs is the vertical jump test.

Procedure Using a Vertec:

1. Stand directly under the extended flags, a comfortable distance from the telescoping post. The reach arm should be closest to the post.

2. Feet should be parallel and planted on the ground. A preparatory step is not allowed. However, bending the knees and swinging the arms prior to the jump is allowed.

3. During the jump, extend the reach arm as high as possible and tap the flags, pushing the highest flag reached away.

4. After a full recovery, allow subsequent trials until the athlete can no longer reach a flag.

5. Record the height of the highest flag moved.

6. Subtract the standing reach value from the vertical jump score to determine the absolute vertical jump:

   VJ (no step) - SR = VJ (no step) TOTAL

Procedure Using a Wall:

1. Extend a yardstick up the wall from the highest reach of the fingertips and attach the yardstick to the wall.

2. Chalk the fingertips of the reach hand.

3. Turn sideways (reach arm is closest to the wall) and jump and reach as high as possible and tap the yardstick with one hand. The athlete may bend the knees prior to the jump, but is not allowed an approach step.

4. Read the number on the yardstick that corresponds with the highest chalk mark.

Note: To more accurately determine the score, the tester should stand on a chair or ladder.

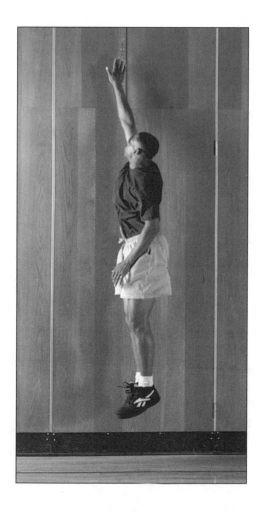

VERTICAL JUMP (ONE STEP)

Purpose: To accurately determine vertical jumping for basketball, which is often the combined by-product of horizontal velocity and vertical lift. Occasions when horizontal momentum transfers to vertical movement in basketball include driving the lane en route to a slam dunk or boxing out during a shot, then quickly stepping and jumping for the rebound. Some players may lack the strength, coordination, flexibility, or capacity to decelerate required for dynamic vertical jumps. By allowing an approach step during the vertical jump test you can more accurately determine your ability to convert speed generated from a horizontal approach to vertical lift, which is a simple measure of transfer of power.

Procedure Using a Vertec:

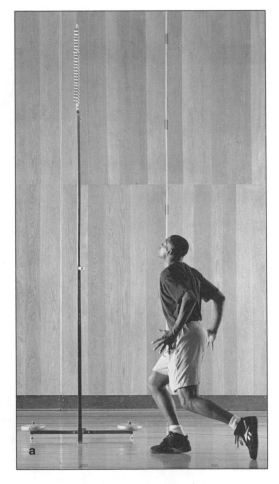

1. Take a position an un-specified distance from the Vertec that was predetermined through practice trials. The reach arm should be closest to the post.

2. Take **one** full stride and a "plant" or "gather" step. This should place the athlete under the flags.

3. During the jump, extend the reach arm as high as possible and tap the flags, pushing away the highest flag reached.

4. After a full recovery, allow subsequent trials until the athlete can no longer reach a flag.

5. Record the highest flag moved.

6. Subtract the standing reach value from the vertical jump score to determine the absolute vertical jump:

VJ (one step) - SR = VJ (one step) TOTAL

Note: Due to potential danger, do not perform this test using the wall protocol.

STANDING LONG JUMP

Purpose: When you jump, you project the body into the air, using force generated by the feet against the ground. Most training regimens emphasize forward, backward, lateral, vertical, and combination movements. To accurately assess explosive effort, your tests must not be limited to measuring power only in the vertical plane. Basketball also requires explosive movement in a horizontal direction. The standing long jump is an ideal test to measure power of the legs in the horizontal plane.

Note: We use a long, folding mat for this test. The protocol is the same as indicated below with the exception of placing a strip of tape on the floor. We simply have the athlete stand with his or her toes touching the edge of the mat. If such a mat is unavailable then use the following protocol.

Procedure:

1. Select a level, unobstructed, semi-resilient surface and place a strip of athletic tape on the floor.

2. Do a couple of practice trials to become familiar with foot placement and jump technique.

3. Take a comfortable position with the toes immediately behind the tape line.

4. Have the tester rub chalk on the athlete's heels.

a

5. The athlete can swing the arms and bend the knees, but a preparatory step is not allowed.

6. Jump forward as far as possible. Upon landing the athlete is not allowed to fall or step back, but may fall forward, if necessary.

7. The chalked heels will leave a distinct mark on the floor. Measure the closest mark to the back of the tape line.

8. Make several attempts and record the best score.

HEXAGON

Purpose: This test was developed by the United States Tennis Association as part of their extensive player assessment program. A basketball player can use the same hexagon test to measure speed, quickness, power, coordination, agility, and dynamic balance. This test challenges you to move with maximum speed while maintaining balance.

Procedure:

1. Using athletic tape, mark a hexagon (24 inches per side) on the floor (each angle will be 120 degrees).

2. Stand with the feet together in the middle of the hexagon facing the front line.

Note: One side of the hexagon is designated the front line. The athlete faces this direction throughout the test.

3. On the command "Get set! Go!" jump ahead across the line and then back over the *same* line into the middle of the hexagon.

4. Then, continuing to face forward with the feet still together, jump over the next side and back into the hexagon. Continue this pattern for three full revolutions. Jump clockwise or counterclockwise. The athlete may want to be tested jumping in both directions to determine if any left or right imbalances exist in his or her movement skills.

5. When the feet enter the hexagon after three complete revolutions, the clock should be stopped and the time noted.

6. A half-second penalty will be assessed each time a line is touched or a jump made out of sequence from the dictated hexagon pattern.

7. Take one practice trial, and then record the best time from two tests.

20-YARD AGILITY RUN

Purpose: Physical maneuverability with minimal sacrifice of time is certainly an advantage when performing most movements in sport. Agility involves upsetting the body's equilibrium to accommodate a rapid and accurate change of position during movement. The 20-yard agility run is a simple measure of acceleration, deceleration, change of direction, and, to a large degree, dynamic flexibility. The test results serve as an important criterion in establishing physical preparation regimens.

Procedure:

1. To set up the 20-yard agility run, select a level, non-slip surface and place a 3-foot length of athletic tape on the floor to serve as a center line. Measure 5 yards in both directions from the center line and place a similar length of tape at these points.

2. Position the tester at the center line.

Tester

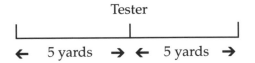

← 5 yards → ← 5 yards →

3. Straddle the center with feet an equal distance apart and parallel to the line. Place a hand on the line (see Figure a).

4. On the command "Get set! Go!" sprint in the direction of choice and touch the first line with the **hand** (see Figure b). Change direction immediately and sprint past the center line to the opposite, or second, line. Touch this line with the **hand**. Again, reverse direction and sprint across the center line to end the test.

Note: Do not touch the center line when finishing.

5. The tester starts the watch on the command "Go" and stops the watch when the torso crosses the center line after both sidelines have been touched.

6. Record the best of 3 trials.

SIT-UPS AND PUSH-UPS

Purpose: Muscular endurance is the capacity of a muscle or group of muscles to sustain repeated contractions. It also refers to the ability of a muscle to apply force and sustain it for a period of time. The sit-up test determines the endurance of the abdominal muscles and hip flexors, while the push-up test will assess the endurance of upper body muscles such as the pectorals, anterior deltoids, and triceps.

Procedure for Sit-Up Test:

1. Lie supine with hips flexed to 45°, knees flexed to 90°, and feet flat on the floor. **No one should hold the feet down**.

2. Cross the arms in front of the body. The hands should touch the shoulders throughout the test.

3. Perform as many sit-ups as possible in 1 minute. To qualify as a complete sit-up

    *   the elbows must touch the knees;

    *   the shoulder blades must touch the mat; and

    *   the hips must stay on the mat.

Note: Any athlete with a history of low back pain or back problems should not perform this test.

Procedure for Push-Up Test:

1. Get in a prone position with the hands shoulder-width apart and the weight of the lower body on the balls of the feet.

2. Start with the arms fully extended and the head, shoulders, back, hips, knees, and ankles in a straight line. Maintain this position throughout the test.

3. Record the number of push-ups successfully completed in 1 minute. To qualify as a complete push-up

   • the upper arm must reach parallel to the floor during the down phase;

   • the arms must be completely extended in the up position; and

   • the straight body alignment must be maintained.

SIT-AND-REACH

Purpose: Flexibility is an important part of successful basketball performance and represents the capacity to move a joint throughout its range of motion. Good flexibility can decrease the chance of injury, muscle soreness, and low back pain. The sit-and-reach test gauges the range of motion at the hip joint and more specifically assesses the flexibility of the hamstrings and lower back muscles. If limitations are discovered, you should begin specific stretching exercises to increase flexibility in this area.

Procedure:

1. Sit with the knees extended and legs flat against the floor. The tester or assistant may need to apply gentle pressure to the knees to ensure that they do not raise off the floor.

2. Put the feet (shoes removed) flat against the test box. Extend the hands out in front of the body with index fingers touching.

3. Lean forward with arms extended (hold for a two count), and measure the distance from the fingertips to the edge of the box (i.e., the bottom of the feet).

4. If the athlete is unable to reach past the feet, the score will be expressed as a negative value. If the athlete is capable of reaching past the feet, the score will be expressed as a positive value.

5. Record the best of 3 trials.

ANAEROBIC FITNESS

Purpose: The explosive nature of basketball, where a player must continually start, stop, and change directions, requires anaerobic work. The better able a player is to perform at a high intensity for a longer duration, the more effective he or she will be on the court.

Note: Several of the court drills in chapters 8 and 9 are ideal to use as field tests to determine anaerobic capacity.

Procedure:

1. Select a drill that requires few basketball variables such as dribbling, shooting, and passing. Drills that involve straight sprinting work the best.

2. The drill should be easy to replicate and last a minimum of 2 minutes. For those drills in which one complete repetition lasts a minute or less, several continuous repetitions should be run. The length of the combined repetitions should range between 2 and 3 minutes.

3. Complete the drill and record the athlete's time.

AEROBIC FITNESS

Purpose: The ability to play at a high intensity, to recover rapidly during free throws, changes of possession, and time-outs, and to still perform effectively at the end of the game, requires a well developed aerobic energy system. Basketball is a game that derives energy primarily from anaerobic sources, however, the aerobic system provides the base from which to build the total conditioning program. Being aerobically fit is characterized by functional efficiency of the heart, lungs, and circulatory system. The time it takes to run 2 miles is an acceptable measure of aerobic fitness. More importantly, the 2-mile test is a measure that should be used periodically to determine gains or losses in your conditioning program throughout the year.

Procedure:

1. Perform a thorough warm-up.

2. On a track, stand behind the start/finish line. An outdoor track measures four laps to the mile; laps per mile vary on indoor tracks, but eight laps per mile is typical.

3. Begin running on the command "Get set! Go!"

4. There should be one timer for each player running. The timer should call out the time and the number of laps remaining each time the athlete runs past the start/finish line.

Note: Many tracks are metric, where four laps equal 1,600 meters or approximately 5,250 feet (1 mile is equal to 5,280 feet). This 30-foot discrepancy (60 feet for 2 miles) is not as important as replicating the same distance on subsequent tests. Record the time at the end of each run.

CHAPTER 7

USING BASKETBALL CONDITIONING DRILLS

Before using or conducting any of the

drills described in this manual, understand that each of the activities has a purpose or multiple purposes. Coaches shouldn't use a drill simply to keep their players busy during practice. Players shouldn't perform a drill simply out of habit or from seeing someone else using the drill. Consider what the drills can do for you and your team.

Most of the drills in this book require a variety of movement patterns. A certain degree of skill is needed to execute these movements correctly. And some of the drills require more skill than others. To use the drills effectively, you must first understand the difference between *technique training* and *conditioning*.

If your purpose for using a drill is to develop movement skills, then the drill should be performed near the beginning of the practice or workout, while you are fresh. Your emphasis would be on using correct movement technique rather than conditioning.

If your purpose for using a drill is to condition the anaerobic or aerobic energy system, then you'd place less emphasis on executing precise movement skills (although you should always try to use correct technique). In this case, the conditioning drills should follow all other technique work.

In selecting conditioning drills, focus on the physiological needs for playing basketball, not on the development of specific basketball skills. However, whenever possible, try to incorporate specific skills such as shooting, passing, and dribbling, not only to improve these techniques, but to add to the challenge of the drill. Always try to perform the skills correctly, but if your primary purpose is to condition, allow for less than perfect execution because of fatigue.

ABOUT THE DRILLS

The court conditioning drills presented in *Complete Conditioning for Basketball* vary in their degree of difficulty and time requirements. You must determine what activities are appropriate for your level of fitness and athletic ability (as determined by the scores from the tests in chapter 6) and for the outcomes you desire.

Consider your personal goals, your team's style of play, your position and role on the team, and what you have the most fun doing. After all, if you don't stay motivated enough to do the drills, it is unlikely you will continue doing them.

Because individual responses and adaptations to conditioning vary among players, avoid comparing your training to that of your teammates. Work at improving **your** fitness and athleticism.

Guidelines for Using Drills

- Select a drill.
- Adapt the drill to fit the facility and equipment available.
- Adjust the drill to your level of fitness.
- Adjust the drill to the number of players who will be involved.
- Most importantly, be creative. The worst thing that can happen is to get turned off to the drills because of boredom.

INDIVIDUAL AND TEAM DRILLS

The drills in this book are divided into two sections. The drills presented in chapter 8, "Individual Drills," are best suited for less than five players per one full court (given the typical space limitations of most practice facilities). The drills in this section are valuable because, by using them, a coach can closely evaluate the movement skills of an individual player. These drills also typically require the player to cover a large portion of the floor or utilize one or both baskets in rapid succession. These drills would, therefore, create congestion and confusion if a large number of players was involved.

The team drills presented in chapter 9 can also be adapted to the needs of individuals, pairs, and small groups of players, but are ideal for entire teams. In team drills, make sure everyone participating knows his or her role and responsibility. This will decrease the chance of confusion and ensure a smooth flow in the drill's execution.

Because of the complexity of most of the drill patterns and because of the involvement of several rebounders and passers per player, make safety a priority when performing the individual drills in chapter 8. The team drills in chapter 9 involve the coordinated effort of many participants in complex movement patterns, and therefore the potential for confusion exists. Choose only those activities that you feel confident you can execute without a mishap.

VARIETY IS THE SPICE OF CONDITIONING DRILLS

Basketball is a sport requiring a variety of movement patterns. Sprinting, back-pedaling, hopping, jumping, back- and side-shuffling are a few of the more important motor skills needed.

In addition, the game of basketball is dynamic, with no two situations exactly alike. Players, match-ups, strategies, time, score, and so on are continually changing. To be an effective player, you have to be able to make adjustments in your thinking and in your movement patterns to meet each unique situation and challenge on the court.

Because basketball involves a variety of movement patterns, your conditioning regimen should include a variety of movement skills that are basketball-related. Especially important for any basketball-specific training program are combination movement patterns performed using the anaerobic energy system.

Incorporating variety in your training will help prepare you for the quick mental adjustments you're required to make during the course of a game. If your mental skills become stagnant from performing the same monotonous drills day in and day out, you'll be less able to make the split-second decisions that often mean the difference between a successful or failed attempt.

Although the format of your conditioning program should remain constant (warm-up/stretch, skill development, conditioning phase, and cool-down), you can incorporate variety through the 50 on-court drills and their variations presented in *Complete Conditioning for Basketball*. By continually varying the drills, you can perform a diversity of basketball skills (dribbling, passing, shooting) while developing your energy systems (anaerobic vs. aerobic) and assorted movement patterns (sprinting, shuffling, skipping, etc.). And the drill variations allow you to use more or fewer players, to develop different movement patterns, and to introduce individual or team competition into the workout.

So, use the many different court drills in this book to improve your conditioning. Be creative and adjust the drills to fit your changing needs as you become a better player and a better-conditioned athlete.

UNDERSTANDING THE DRILL FORMAT AND TERMS

The design of the drills may take some getting used to. But once you're familiar with the symbols (see "Key to Drills") and how they're presented to explain the actions and sequence of the drills, you'll find the drills very easy to understand.

Following the "Key to Drills" is "Terminology at a Glance" (pp. 114-117) summarizing the basic and supplementary fundamental movement patterns (see chapter 5), as well as definitions of other terms used in the drills.

Key to Drills

①   A circled number indicates that some action will take place at that spot.
Action examples:
- Start/stop point
- Jump shot
- Dunk/power lay-up
- Rim/backboard tap
- Execute pass
- Receive pass/intercept pass
- Quick jumps over lines

1-2   Numbers indicate a spot on the court where a player is positioned or where a player will move to. In the diagrams, many numbers are positioned close to, but do not actually touch, a point of reference such as the basket, sideline, baseline, center circle, and so on. The drill should be fully executed to the point of reference (i.e., the athlete should touch the sideline with the foot, etc.). Movements might involve sprinting, power shuffle, back-pedal, and so on.

———→   Indicates direction of a movement (sprint, power shuffle, etc.).

— — — ➤   Indicates a pass.

〰〰➤   Indicates a dribble or a drive to the basket.

Ⓟ   Indicates the spot where the coach or nonworking player stands to pass the ball to the working player(s).

Ⓡ   Indicates a rebounder or rebounder/passer—a coach or a nonworking player who must rebound and/or pass the ball to the working player(s). The rebounder may be required to sprint the floor prior to delivering a pass.

Ⓒ   Indicates the spot where the coach stands to direct the drill or pass the ball.

[X]   Indicates the approximate spot for placement of a cone.

★   Indicates the approximate spot that a working player will receive a pass.

A   A letter indicates an individual player when multiple working players are involved in a drill.

A1   A letter with a number differentiates positions of different working players.

Ⓐ1   A circled letter and/or a letter with a number differentiates actions performed by different working players.

Terminology at a Glance

Back-Pedal: Typically a defensive move (quick run, opposite direction the player is facing).

- Body's center of gravity is <u>low.</u>

- Stride length is <u>short.</u>

- Stride frequency is <u>fast.</u>

Back Shuffle or Defensive Slide: A defensive move, backward.

- Body's center of gravity is <u>low.</u>

- Back is straight.

- Knees are bent.

- Upper torso and head are stationary and facing opposite the direction of travel.

- Lead foot is perpendicular to the trailing foot (and therefore also perpendicular to the direction of travel).

- Trailing foot is pointing opposite the direction of travel.

- Arms and hands are in the defensive, "ready" position.

Note: All movement is generated with the lower abdominals and lower body. Pick up the lead foot, push with the trailing foot, plant and pull with the lead foot—Repeat.

Back Sprint: "Sprinting" backward. When the objective is to move from point A to point B as rapidly as possible, backward. Typically a defensive move.

- Body's center of gravity is <u>high</u> (similar to normal, forward sprinting).

- Stride length is <u>long.</u>

- Stride frequency is slightly <u>slower</u> than Back-Pedal.

Back Shuffle-Pivot: Same body position and action as described in Back Shuffle above, however, the player will reverse pivot (pivot on the lead foot) after every second step and slide. Only the lower body pivots. The upper torso and head remain stationary and facing opposite the direction of travel.

Carioca:	A movement pattern designed to enhance agility, quickness, coordination, and body control **(For description purposes the athlete is moving to his/her right).**

- Arms and hands are in the defensive, "ready" position.

- Upper torso and head is stationary and facing 90 degrees to the direction of travel.

- Lead foot (right foot) is slightly pointed in the direction of travel.

Note: All movement is from the lower body.

Action: 1. *Cross behind*—step behind the lead foot with the left foot.
2. *Side step*—"drive" off the left foot and step in the direction of travel with the lead foot.
3. *Cross in front*—"plant" the lead foot. Forcefully "drive" the left knee across in front of the lead leg. Athlete should try to cover as much ground as possible on the *cross in front* step.
4. *Side step*—following the cross in front step, "plant" and "drive off" the left foot and step with the lead foot in the direction of travel.
5. *Repeat*—1 through 4 above.

Drive/Dribble:	A scenario frequently encountered during many of the drills is a player who receives a pass while sprinting toward a basket. It is the prerogative of the coach, or the player, to either *dribble* or simply *carry* the ball to the basket.
Dunk/Power Lay-Up:	If the athlete is capable, an explosive move culminating with a slam dunk would be exceptional. However, for most players, a strong move to the basket ending with a lay-up is acceptable and would constitute a *power lay-up*.
Jumper:	Player shoots a jump shot.
Power Shuffle (Step Slide):	A lateral, defensive move (For description purposes the athlete is moving to his/her right).

- Arms and hands are in a defensive "ready" position.

- Upper torso and head is stationary and facing 90 degrees to the direction of travel.

- Low center of gravity. Bend at the knees, not at the waist.

- Lead foot (right foot) is slightly pointed in the direction of travel.

Action: 1. *Step*—Simultaneously pick up the lead foot (exaggerate lead leg knee drive), and explosively push with the trailing foot.

2. *Slide*—Plant the right foot and *slide* the trailing foot to, but do not cross, the lead foot.

Note: Unlike a fast, "choppy" defensive slide, the Power Shuffle should incorporate an explosive stride while maintaining a quick frequency.

Repetitions: An individual full cycle of an exercise or one complete movement of a drill.

Rim/Backboard Taps: An activity in which the athlete repeatedly jumps and touches the rim, backboard, net or any suspended object (simply jumping in place and reaching would suffice). The leaping ability of the athlete dictates how high he/she will jump. Emphasis is placed *on how quick* the athlete jumps, not how *high*.

Round Trips Per Set: Used for description purposes, several drills make reference to "round trips" rather than repetitions. Used only for drills where the start and stop point is the same spot. During the continuation of a drill each time the start and stop point is crossed, one "round trip" is counted.

Sets: A distinct grouping of repetitions or round trips followed by a rest interval and then subsequent sets. Usually several sets are performed for each drill.

Skipping, High-Knee Running, Running With Hands Above Head, Heel Kicks: Examples of fundamental movement patterns that may replace sprinting or jogging during some aspect of specific drills. Facilitates variety and inhibits monotony. Partial listing of movement patterns:
Skipping—Similar to normal skipping, however, exaggerate arm action, knee lift, and stride length.
High-Knee Running—Exaggerated knee lift, mechanical arm action, short, quick, stride.
Running With Hands Above Head—Eliminate the use of the arms by placing the hands on the head. This increases the work demand for the legs.
Heel Kicks—Shoulder, hip, knee, and ankle are in a straight line when the foot is on the ground. Tempo is fast, no knee lift, heel should touch the buttocks.

Sprint:	To run fast over a short distance. Two mechanical variables influence speed: stride length and stride frequency. An athlete's goal is to maximize both variables.
	• Cyclic leg action—explosive knee lift and "drive phase" *quick* off the ground (support phase).
	• The rotary action of the legs evoke a contrary reaction with the arms (*left* arm "drives" forward simultaneously with the *right* knee lift).
Variation:	Different options that may be incorporated into the described drill pattern. Variations might include
	• using multiple players, balls, cones, and so on;
	• adjusting the pattern to accommodate larger numbers of athletes;
	• developing different movement patterns; and
	• team and player competitions.
	Note: Coaches and athletes are encouraged to create their own variations.

CHAPTER 8

INDIVIDUAL DRILLS

The following 25 court drills and their variations work best for individuals, pairs, or small groups of players. The drills require sufficient space for proper execution of movement, shooting, passing, and rebounding skills. These drills are more effective and safer for individuals and small groups who can keep the flow going and create little congestion.

Examine each drill closely. Make sure you fully understand the movement patterns required, the intensity and duration of the drill, the number of balls and the number of passers and rebounders involved, and any other important considerations. And be creative! Athletes and coaches with whom I work have helped me develop many of the drill variations you'll find in this book.

INDIVIDUAL 1

(1)   Start under the basket facing the near baseline

1-2   Back shuffle/defensive slide—left foot leads

2-3   Sprint

3-4   Power shuffle (1-2 steps)—facing the near baseline

4-5   Back shuffle/defensive slide—right foot leads

5-6   Sprint

6-7   Power shuffle (1-2 steps)—facing the near baseline

(7)   Repeat

Note: If multiple players are involved, after the first player performs for a set time (15 to 60 seconds) or makes a predetermined number of round trips, the next player immediately rotates to the active position.
*Depending on the training emphasis, typically three players per lane is ideal. With a little practice, two and even three players per lane can perform the drill simultaneously.

Variations:

1. Start with three rim/backboard taps. Power shuffle from position 1 to 3, back-pedal from position 3 to 2, sprint from position 2 to 4, and do three rim/backboard taps. Repeat on the opposite side.

2. Using two or more baskets, try individual or team races.

3. Coach calls out a position number. The player power shuffles, back shuffle/defensive slides, back-pedals, or sprints to the designated position. The position of the player and the number called dictate the movement pattern. (For example, the player begins at position 1, the coach calls "5," and the player back shuffles/defensive slides to position 5; the coach calls "2," the player power shuffles to position 2; the coach calls "1," the player sprints to position 1; the coach calls "3," the player power shuffles to position 3; and so on.)

INDIVIDUAL 1

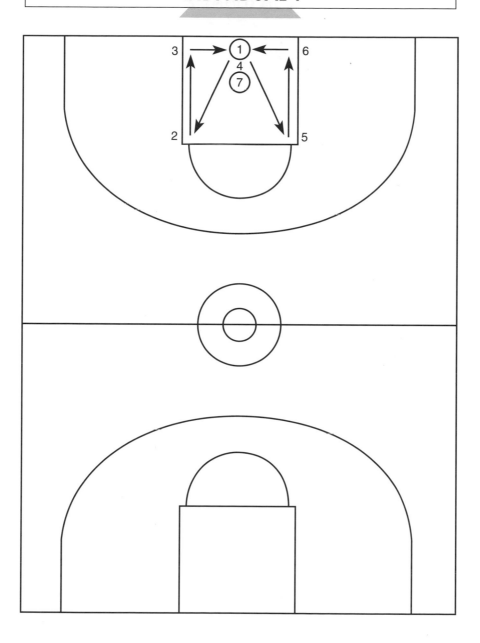

INDIVIDUAL 2

(1) Start

1-2 Power shuffle

2-3 Power shuffle

Continue

Note: Perform drill for 30 seconds to 1 minute.

*Emphasize a "low" shuffle with an explosive stride.

Variations:

1. Power shuffle only—three to four steps to cross the lane.

2. The player faces the passer—every 5 to 10 seconds the ball is passed and the player spins, performs a dunk/power lay-up, rebounds, passes the ball back to the passer, and immediately continues to shuffle.

3. Same as variation 2 except the player is facing the near basket. On voice command from the passer the player spins, catches the pass, spins back to the basket, performs a dunk/power lay-up, rebounds, passes the ball back to the passer, and immediately continues to shuffle.

INDIVIDUAL 2

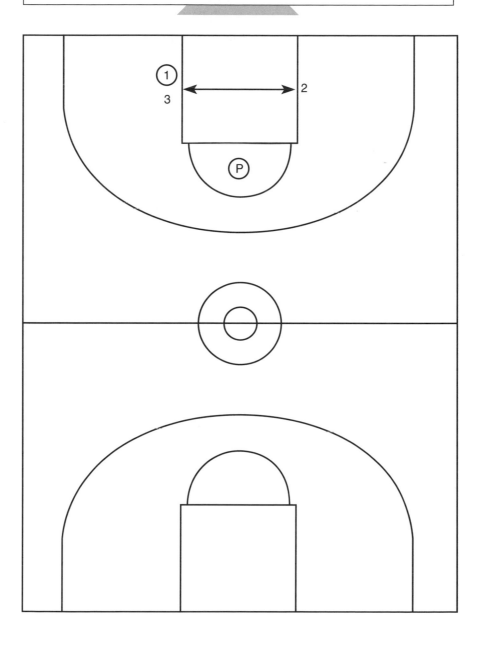

INDIVIDUAL 3

(1)   Start under the basket—perform five rim/backboard taps

1-2   Low power shuffle

2-3   Low power shuffle

3-4   Low power shuffle

4-5   Low power shuffle

5-6   Low power shuffle

6-7   Low power shuffle

7-8   Low power shuffle

(8)   Five rim/backboard taps

Repeat

Variations:

1. Vary the movement patterns. Sprinting and high-knee running work great. **Note:** High-knee running can be extremely demanding.

2. Follow the same number sequence listed above, but every time the player crosses the basket, have the player perform three to five rim/backboard taps.
   Note: Again, vary the movement patterns.

3. This is an excellent drill for the entire team. Space the players evenly down the sideline. Eliminate the rim taps. Cones are helpful to indicate "turn-around" spots for those players working in the middle of the court.

INDIVIDUAL 3

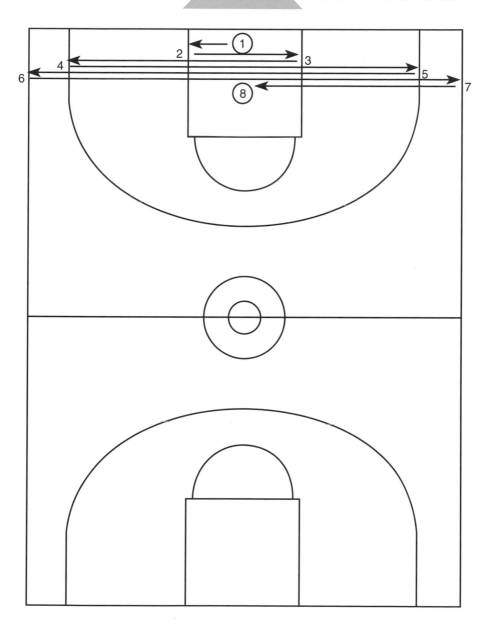

INDIVIDUAL 4

(1) Start

1-2 Sprint—receive pass at ★, drive to the basket

(2) Dunk/power lay-up

2-3 Power shuffle—face the opposite baseline

3-4 Sprint—receive pass at ★, drive to the basket

(4) Dunk/power lay-up

4-5 Power shuffle—face the opposite baseline

(5) Repeat

Note: Rebounder sprints the length of the court and passes to the player for a fast break dunk/power lay-up.

*Perform 1 to 10 round trips per set clockwise, then repeat the same number of sets counterclockwise.

Variations:

1. Shoot a jumper from the elbow instead of the dunk/power lay-up.

2. An interesting variation is to alternate the rebounder with the player performing the lay-up. For example, player A sprints from position 1 to 2 and executes a dunk/power lay-up, but rather than power shuffling from position 2 to 3, player A retrieves the rebound and sprints up the middle of the court. After player B (the rebounder who was sprinting up the center of the court while player A was sprinting from position 1 to 2) passes to player A, he or she continues on toward the baseline rather than rebounding the ball. Player B then power shuffles from position 2 to 3, sprints from position 3 to 4, receives a pass from player A, and performs a dunk/power lay-up. Make sure the players communicate under the baskets to avoid a collision.

INDIVIDUAL 4

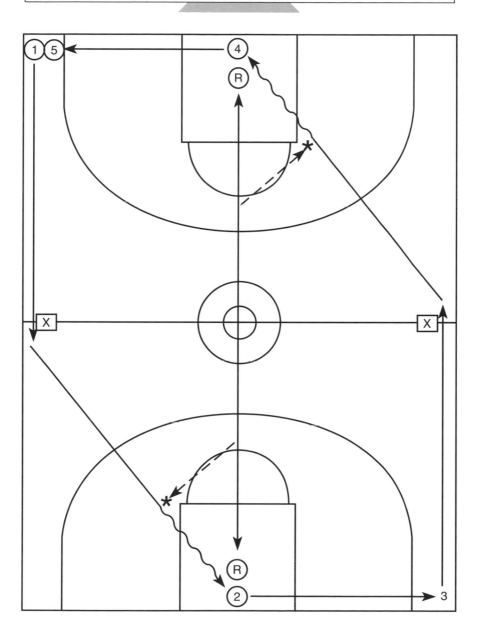

INDIVIDUAL 5

(1)   Start at the half-court/sideline junction

1-2   Sprint—receive pass at ★, drive to the basket

(2)   Dunk/power lay-up

2-3   Sprint

3-4   Sprint—receive pass at ★, drive to the basket

(4)   Dunk/power lay-up

4-5   Sprint

(5)   Repeat

Note: Rebounder passes to player at ★.

Variations:

1. The rebounder can vary the pass (roll the ball, make a high toss, etc.).

2. Have the player shoot a jumper from the elbow. The player should still sprint to the baseline (under the basket) before sprinting to position 3.

3. Evenly space five cones along the half-court line. At the first cone, perform the same pattern outlined above. However, following the dunk/power lay-up, the player should sprint back to the next cone in line. The player continues down the line of cones and back to the start.

INDIVIDUAL 5

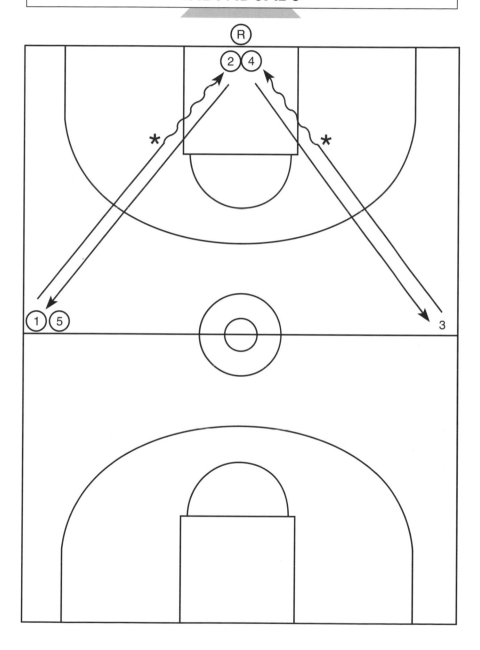

INDIVIDUAL 6

①   Start under the basket—perform three rim/backboard taps

1-2   Sprint

2-3   Sprint

③   Three rim/backboard taps

3-4   Sprint

4-5   Sprint

⑤   Three rim/backboard taps

5-6   Sprint

6-7   Sprint—receive pass at ★, drive to the basket

⑦   Dunk/power lay-up

Variations:

1. Coaches can challenge athletes by setting this drill up as a team relay. Divide the basket in half and have two teams per basket.

2. This is an excellent drill to incorporate a variety of movement patterns. For example, the athlete back-pedals from position 1 to 2 and sprints back to the basket, or power shuffles both directions (from position 1 to 2, position 2 to 3, position 3 to 4, and so on).

3. To make this drill more demanding, try using both baskets. The pattern should be as follows:

   1-2 Sprint to the near free-throw line

   2-3 Sprint back to the basket—perform three rim/backboard taps

   3-4 Sprint to the opposite basket—perform three rim/backboard taps

Repeat steps 1 through 4 in the opposite direction. Players should now be back under the basket where they started. Continue, only this time sprint to the three-point line instead of the free-throw line. Repeat on both ends of the court.

Note: Eliminate the pass and dunk/power lay-up.

INDIVIDUAL 6

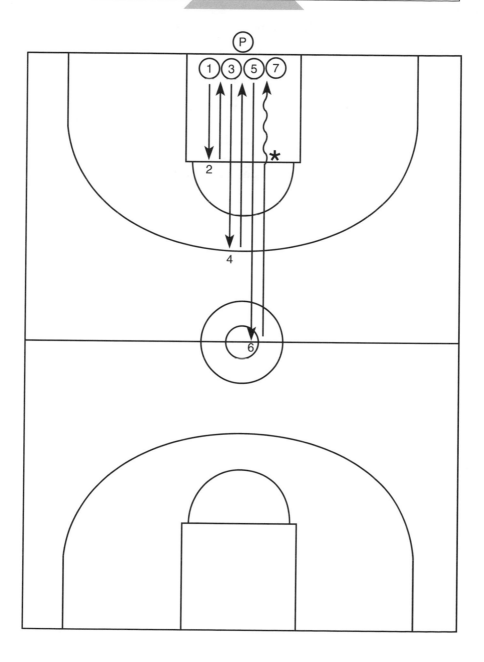

INDIVIDUAL 7

Clockwise run—catch with the left hand only

Counterclockwise run—catch with the right hand only

Clockwise run—catch with the right hand only

Counterclockwise run—catch with the left hand only

Note: 15 to 30 seconds per set or a predetermined number of round trips.
*No rest between sets.
*Player catches and throws using one hand only.
*Player maintains a quick tempo.

Variation:

This is a good warm-up drill. The passer should vary the passes (i.e., pass high, pass low, bounce pass, pass in front and behind the runner).

INDIVIDUAL 7

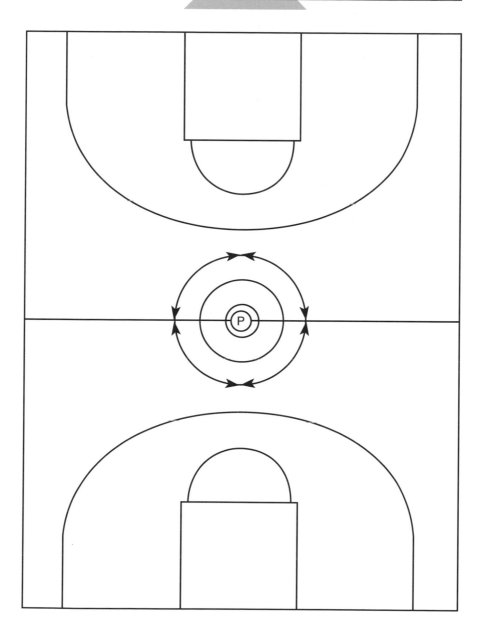

INDIVIDUAL 8

①   Start at the elbow—shoot a jumper

1-2   Sprint

2-3   Sprint—receive pass at the elbow

③   Jumper

3-4   Sprint

4-5   Sprint—receive pass at the elbow

⑤   Jumper

     Repeat

Note: Rebounder passes to player at the elbow.

Variations:

1. Perform the drill for a set time.
2. Perform the drill for a predetermined number of shots.
3. For an added challenge, try playing a "plus one, minus two" game. The game is played to 10. If a player makes a shot, the player receives one point; if a player misses a shot, then two points are deducted from his or her score. Novice shooters should play a "plus one, minus one" game. Otherwise the game might never end.

INDIVIDUAL 8

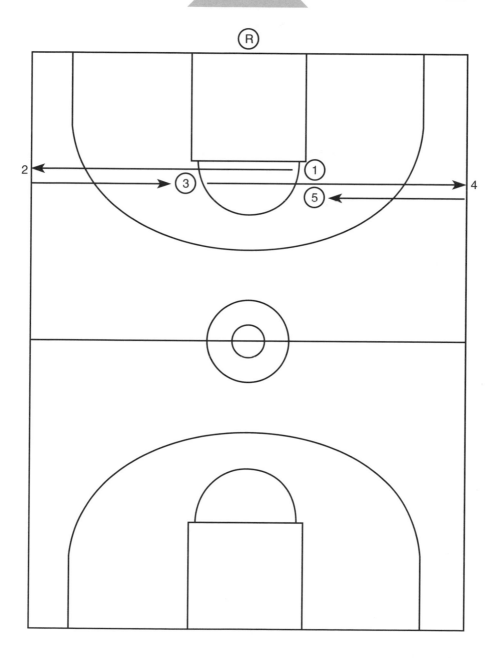

INDIVIDUAL 9

(1) Start—shoot a jumper from the deep corner

1-2 Sprint

2-3 Sprint

3-4 Sprint

(4) 5 to 10 rim/backboard taps

4-5 Sprint—receive pass as approaching deep corner

(5) Jumper

Repeat in the opposite direction

Note: Rebounder passes to player at deep corner spot.
*Movement from position 1 to 5 and from position 5 back to 1 equals one complete repetition. There should be several repetitions per set.

Variations:

1. Vary the movement patterns (power shuffle, back-pedal, back shuffle/defensive slide, etc.). These movements will more accurately resemble a defensive transition.

2. Incorporate two balls and two rebounder/passers. The player shoots from position 1 and sprints toward position 2. A second rebounder/passer is waiting under the basket. As the player approaches, the rebounder/passer passes to the player who then performs a dunk/power lay-up. The player continues the pattern from position 2 to 3 and from position 3 to 4. Again receiving a pass for a dunk/power lay-up (eliminate the rim/backboard taps), the player then sprints to position 5 and repeats in the opposite direction.

3. To involve up to four players, stagger the start (e.g., player B starts when player A reaches position 2). From position 5, each player jogs along the baseline to position 1 and awaits the start of subsequent repetitions.

4. The same pattern can be shortened to half-court. Instead of sprinting to the far baseline, back to half-court, and then to the baseline, the player turns around at half-court, sprints to the near free-throw line, and back to center court.

INDIVIDUAL 9

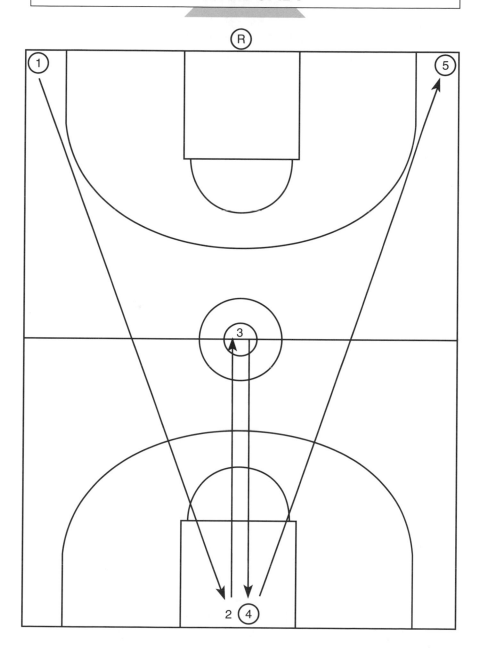

INDIVIDUAL 10

(1)　Start under the basket facing the near baseline

1-2　Power shuffle—facing the near baseline

2-3　Power shuffle—facing the near baseline

3-4　Back-pedal

4-5　Back shuffle/defensive slide—left foot leads

(5)　Intercept pass at ★

5-6　Sprint—drive to the basket

(6)　Dunk/power lay-up

6-7　Power shuffle—facing the near baseline

7-8　Power shuffle—facing the near baseline

8-9　Back-pedal

9-10　Back shuffle/defensive slide—right foot leads

(10)　Intercept pass at ★

10-11　Sprint—drive to the basket

(11)　Dunk/power lay-up

　　　Repeat

Note: Rebounder passes an "outlet," which is intercepted at ★.
*Quick transitions between movements (shuffle, back-pedal, back shuffle/defensive slide, etc.).

Variations:

1. Often I'll throw or roll the ball nearly the full length of the court and require the player to turn, sprint, and chase down the ball before it goes out-of-bounds. The player then drives the length of the floor for a dunk/power lay-up.

2. I have also incorporated a defender into the drill pattern. Player A is facing the passer, the basket, and player B. The movement patterns described above remain the same. Player B mirrors player A (note: player B jogs while player A is back-pedaling, so player B must be careful not to trip player A). The passer throws the ball downcourt. Player A, still facing the passer, has first advantage and sprints to the ball. Player B defends player A's drive to the basket.

INDIVIDUAL 10

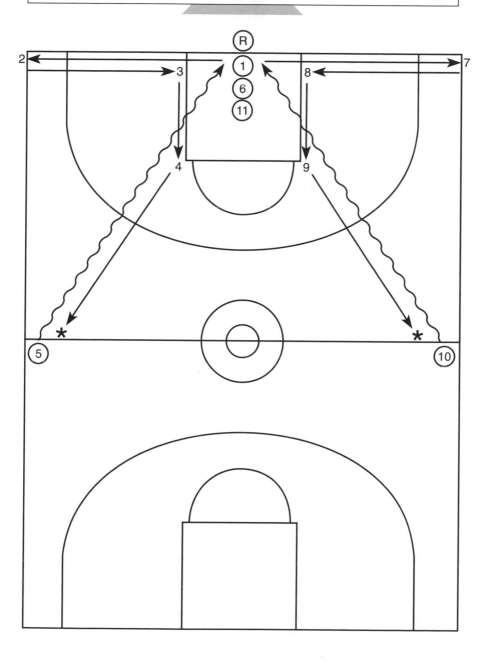

INDIVIDUAL 11

(1) Start at the elbow—shoot a jumper

1-2 Back-pedal

2-3 Power shuffle—facing the near baseline

3-4 Sprint—receive pass at ★, drive to the basket

(4) Dunk/power lay-up

4-5 Power shuffle—facing the near baseline

5-6 Back-pedal

6-7 Sprint—receive pass at the elbow

(7) Jumper

7-8 Back-pedal

8-9 Power shuffle—facing the near baseline

9-10 Sprint—receive pass at ★, drive to the basket

(10) Dunk/power lay-up

10-11 Power shuffle—facing the near baseline

11-12 Back-pedal

12-13 Sprint—receive pass at the elbow

(13) Jumper

Repeat

Note: Repeat two to five round trips per set.

*Quick transitions between movements (shuffle, back-pedal, sprint, etc.).

Variations:

1. To make this more of a shooting drill, try the following pattern: Shoot a jumper at position 1, back-pedal from position 1 to 2, power shuffle from position 2 to 3, sprint from position 3 to 1, shoot a jumper at position 1. Continue for several repetitions per set. Repeat on the opposite side.

2. Same as variation 1, but isolate the dunk/power lay-up portion of the drill. Start at position 4, power shuffle from position 4 to 11, back-pedal from position 11 to 12, sprint from position 12 to 4. Receive pass at ★, drive to the basket for a dunk/power lay-up. Continue for several repetitions per set. Repeat on the opposite side.

INDIVIDUAL 11

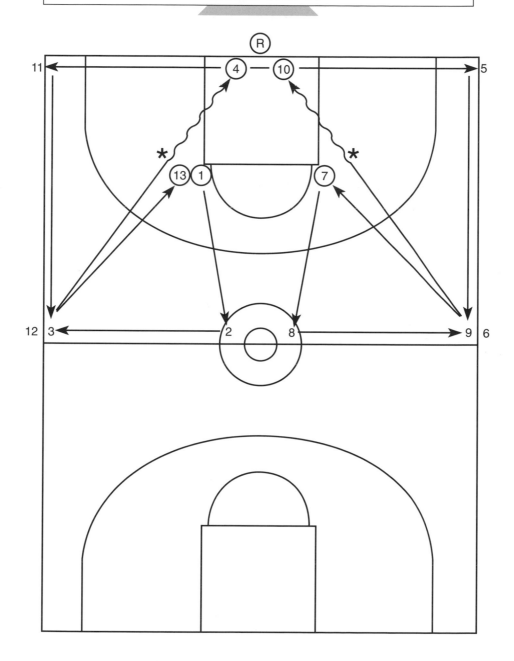

INDIVIDUAL 12

①	Start at the top of the key—shoot a jumper
1-2	Sprint
2-3	Sprint
3-4	Sprint
4-5	Back shuffle/defensive slide—left foot leads
5-6	Sprint
6-7	Back shuffle/defensive slide—right foot leads
7-8	Sprint
8-9	Back-pedal or sprint
9-10	Sprint
⑩	Jumper
	Repeat

Variations:

1. For a fast-pass drill, the same pattern can be performed using only half the court.

2. This is a good drill for a two-player competition (note: one rebounder/passer per player). On the coach's command, two players shoot a jumper from the top of the key. The movement patterns are the same as above; however, make sure the players back shuffle/defensive slide (from position 4 to 5 and from position 6 to 7) in opposition to one another. The first player to make the second jumper (at position 10) wins. If a player misses the final shot, he or she must rebound the ball, sprint back to position 10 and continue shooting/rebounding until the shot has been made.

INDIVIDUAL 12

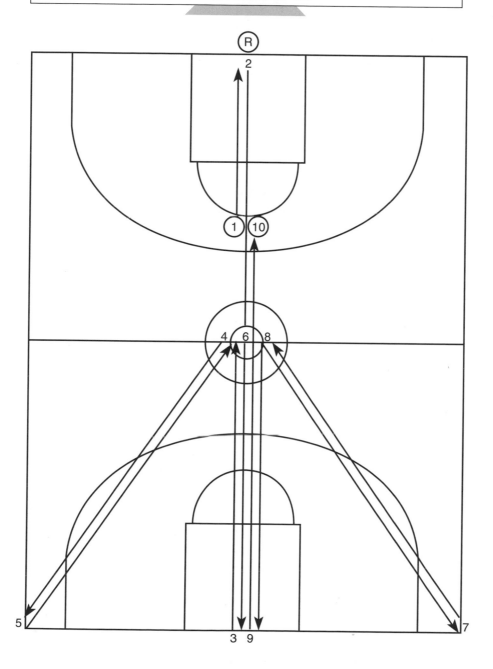

INDIVIDUAL 13

(1) Start under the basket—perform three rim/backboard taps

1-2 Power shuffle—facing the near baseline

2-3 Sprint—receive pass at the elbow

(3) Jumper

3-4 Back shuffle/defensive slide—right foot leads

4-5 Sprint—receive pass at the top of the key

(5) Jumper

5-6 Sprint to the basket

(6) Three rim/backboard taps

6-7 Power shuffle—facing the near baseline

7-8 Sprint—receive pass at the elbow

(8) Jumper

8-9 Back shuffle/defensive slide—left foot leads

9-10 Sprint—receive pass at the top of the key

(10) Jumper

10-11 Sprint to the basket

(11) Three rim/backboard taps

End or repeat

Variation:

If working with two or more players, have player A continually run from position 1 through to position 6 while player B runs the pattern from position 6 through position 11. (Note: There should be one rebounder/ passer per player.) After a set number of repetitions, players switch sides and repeat. Using a 1:2 work-rest ratio, one could easily accommodate six players per half-court. A 30-second rotation would be as follows:

Players A1 and A2: Run

Players B1 and B2: Rebound/pass

Players C1 and C2: Rest

Rotation: A to B, B to C, C to A

Switch to the other side of the basket and repeat.

INDIVIDUAL 13

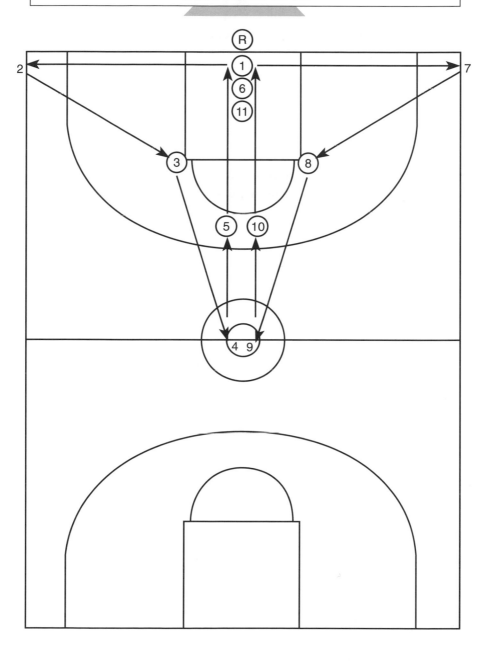

INDIVIDUAL 14

(1) Start at the elbow—shoot a jumper

1-2   Sprint

2-3   Sprint

(3) Jumper—from the elbow

3-4   Power shuffle

4-5   Sprint

(5) Jumper—from the elbow

5-6   Back shuffle/defensive slide—left foot leads

6-7   Sprint—receive pass at ★, drive to the basket

(7) Dunk/power lay-up

7-8   Sprint

8-9   Sprint

9-10 Sprint

10-11 Sprint

(11) Jumper—from the elbow

11-12 Sprint

12-13 Sprint

(13) Jumper—from the elbow

13-14 Power shuffle

14-15 Sprint

(15) Jumper—from the elbow

15-16 Back shuffle/defensive slide—right foot leads

16-17 Sprint—receive pass at ★, drive to the basket

(17) Dunk/power lay-up

End

Note: Two players can perform this drill simultaneously in opposition (two rebounder/passers would be required).

Variation:

The same pattern can be shortened to half-court. Instead of sprinting to the far baseline, then to half-court and back to the baseline, have the player turn around at half-court, then sprint to the near free-throw line and back to half-court.

INDIVIDUAL 14

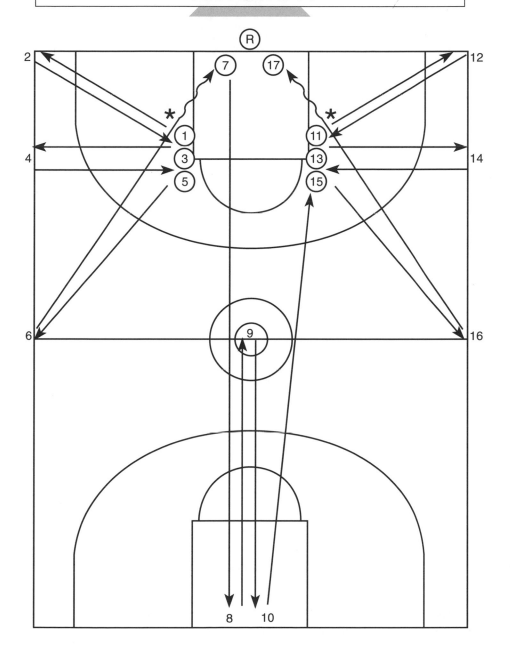

INDIVIDUAL 15

① Start at center court

1-2 Sprint

② Jumper

2-3 Sprint to the basket—perform 1 rim/backboard tap

3-4 Sprint—curl

④ Jumper

4-5 Sprint to the basket—perform 1 rim/backboard tap

5-6 Sprint—curl

⑥ Jumper

6-7 Sprint to the basket—perform 1 rim/backboard tap

7-8 Sprint—curl

⑧ Jumper

8-9 Sprint to the basket—perform 1 rim/backboard tap

9-10 Sprint—curl

⑩ Jumper

10-11 Sprint to the basket—perform 1 rim/backboard tap

11-12 Sprint to center court

12-13 Sprint

⑬ Jumper

13-23 Repeat pattern in reverse

㉓ End at center court

Note: The reason the player "curls" out to the shooting spot is to simulate "coming off a pick."
*Two players can perform this drill simultaneously in opposition (two rebounder/passers would be required).

Variation:

Incorporate various movement patterns such as power shuffle, back shuffle/defensive slide, and back-pedal. However, always sprint to the basket.

INDIVIDUAL 15

INDIVIDUAL 16

(1)   Start at center court

1-2   Sprint—receive pass at the top of the key

(2)   Jumper

2-3   Back shuffle/defensive slide—left foot leads

3-4   Sprint—receive pass at the top of the key

(4)   Jumper

4-5   Back shuffle/defensive slide—right foot leads

5-6   Sprint—receive pass at the top of the key

(6)   Jumper

6-7   Sprint

7-8   Sprint—receive pass at the top of the key

(8)   Jumper

8-9   Sprint

9-10   Sprint—receive pass at the top of the key

(10)   Jumper

10-11 Sprint to center court

(11)   End or repeat

Note: Three players per half-court is ideal. (Incorporate a passer and rotate player to rebounder to passer.)

Variations:

1. Race—have three players on each team with two teams per half-court. Therefore, players must communicate to avoid collisions.

2. Try a timed competition with a half-second penalty for a missed shot.

INDIVIDUAL 16

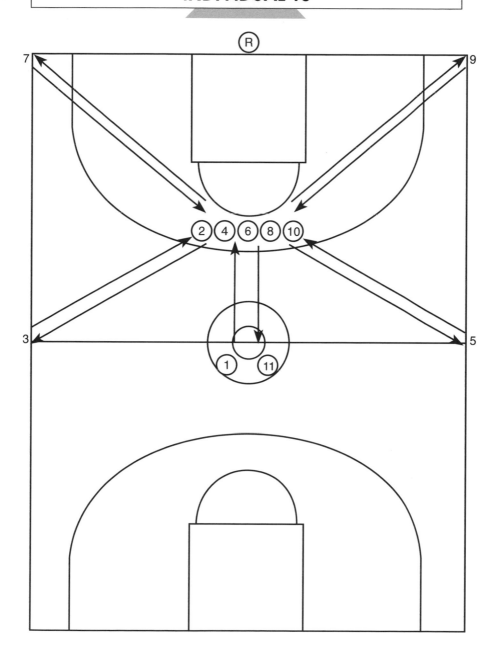

INDIVIDUAL 17

(1)   Start with a jumper

1-2   Sprint

2-3   Sprint—receive pass at ★, drive to the basket

(3)   Dunk/power lay-up

3-4   Back-pedal

4-5   Sprint

(5)   Jumper

     Repeat in the opposite direction

Note: Movement from position 1 to 5 and from position 5 back to 1 equals one complete repetition. There should be several repetitions per set.

Variations:

1. Rather than a dunk/power lay-up, have the rebounder/passer pass to the player at the top of the key. The player shoots a jumper and then continues on with the drill pattern.

2. This is another drill that would be great as a team relay and would accommodate a large number of players. Two balls are required. When player A shoots from position 5, player B starts. The first team to have all players complete the 1 to 5 rotation wins. Players must make the jump shot before continuing. Use one team per half-court.

3. To involve more players, stagger the start. Player B starts after player A shoots from position 5. Player A simply jogs along the baseline to position 1 and awaits the start of subsequent repetitions.

INDIVIDUAL 17

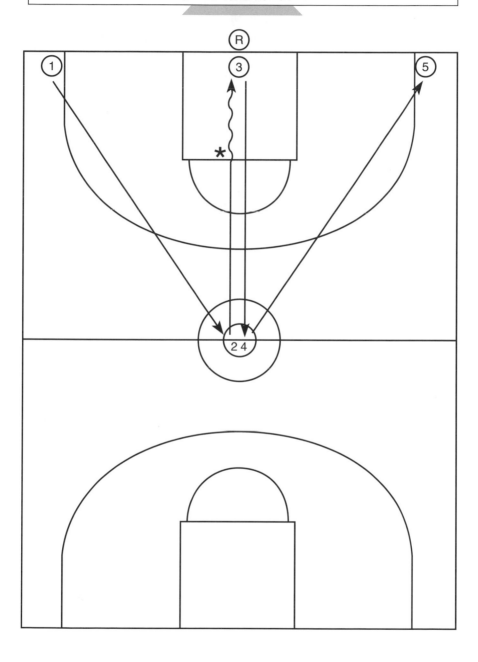

INDIVIDUAL 18

Three players run a figure-8 weave. The ball is handed from player to player as they cross the middle of the "8." On the coach's command, all three players sprint to the basket and immediately start a "tip" drill (ball does not hit the floor).

Note: Quick cuts on the figure-8.
   *15 seconds to 1 minute during the figure-8.
   *15 to 30 seconds during the "tip" drill.

Variation:

Vary the size of the figure-8. Use a tight weave for quick cuts. Use an elongated weave for more running.

INDIVIDUAL 18

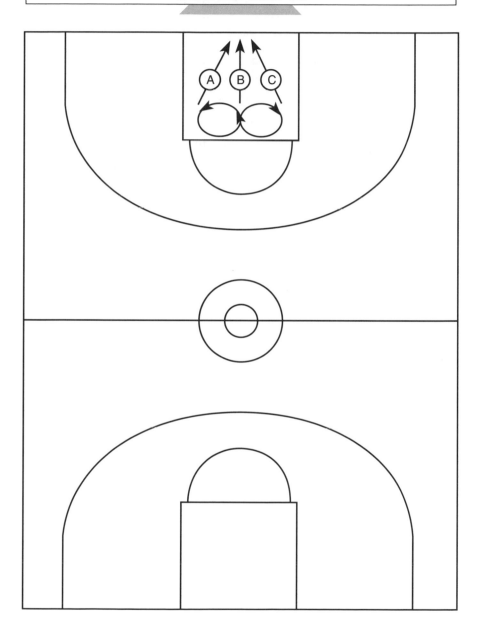

INDIVIDUAL 19

(C) Coach points—forward, back, left, right

All three players (facing coach) simultaneously shuffle, sprint, or back-pedal in the direction the coach is pointing

(C) Coach continues changing direction for 5 to 15 seconds

(C) Coach slaps the ball and passes to one of the players (for description purposes the ball was passed to player A)

Players B and C move to defend against player A while A drives for a lay-up

(C) Coach rebounds the ball

Players A, B, and C immediately return to line and the drill continues

Note: Drill continues for 1 to 2 minutes; next group rotates into position.

Variations:

1. All three players face away from the coach and the basket. Instead of a visual cue (e.g., the coach pointing), the players must respond to an auditory cue. The coach calls out "forward," "back," "right," or "left." After 5 to 15 seconds, the coach calls out "ball" and tosses or rolls the ball toward half-court. All three players must turn and locate the ball. The first player to retrieve the ball drives to the basket. The other two players defend. Continue as described above.

2. Try using four players with two teams of two. When the ball is tossed, the team that gets to it first is on offense and the other team must defend.

INDIVIDUAL 19

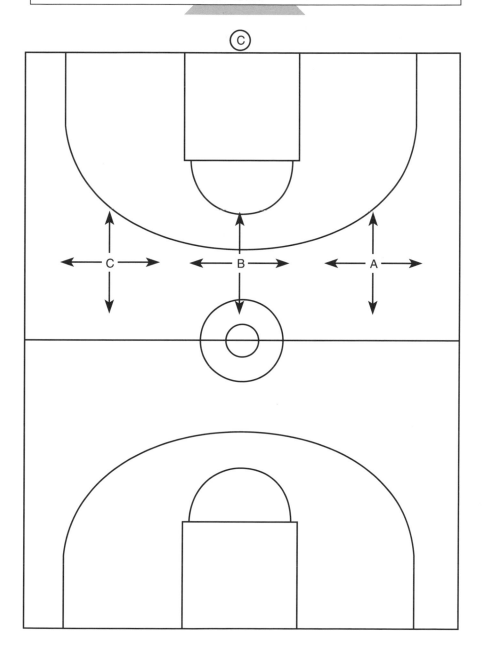

INDIVIDUAL 20

(★1) Approximate spot to receive pass *from* rebounder/passer

(★2) Approximate spot to pass *to* approaching player

(1) Player A starts at the elbow—shoots a jumper

1-2 Player A sprints

2-3 Player A sprints

(★1) Player A receives pass from rebounder/passer

(★2) Player A passes to player B at the elbow (player B is approaching position 1)

Player B shoots jumper and sprints to position 2

Player A continues sprinting to position 3

3-4 Player A sprints and receives pass at the elbow from player B (who is sprinting toward position 3)

(4) Player A shoots a jumper

Repeat

Note: Perform drill for a set time or for a predetermined number of shots. When time or shots have been completed, rest, then repeat on the opposite side.

Variations:

1. Vary the shooting positions (top of the key, three-point line, etc.).

2. For a more advanced and faster paced drill, incorporate a third player and two basketballs.

INDIVIDUAL 20

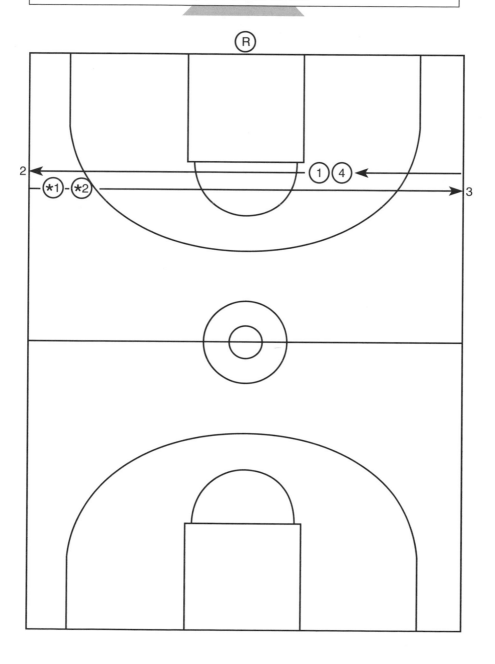

INDIVIDUAL 21

(1)   Start—player A taps the ball to the backboard three times, then passes the ball to player B

1-2   Player A sprints

2-3   Player A sprints and receives pass at the elbow from player B

(3)   Player A shoots a jumper

After player B passes to player A, player B sprints to rebound player A's jumper and continues the process

3-4   Player A sprints and assumes player B's role (see above)

Repeat

Note: Perform drill for a set time or predetermined number of shots. When time or shots have been completed, repeat on the opposite side. *Four players per half-court (two players right, two players left).

Variations:

1. Vary the shooting spots (top of the key, three-point line, etc.) and the distance of the run from position 1 to 2 (three-point line, half-court, opposite three-point line, etc.).

2. If dealing with large numbers of players, you can incorporate a third player. Start with player A at position 1, player B at position 4, and player C at position 2 (it works best if position 2 is moved back to half-court). Player A passes to player B and then sprints to position 2. Player C sprints to position 3 and receives a pass from player B. Player B sprints to position 1 to rebound. Player C shoots a jumper and sprints to position 4. Continue the drill pattern.

Note: Using this variation, you can work six players per half-court. Place three players on each side of the basket, then switch.

INDIVIDUAL 21

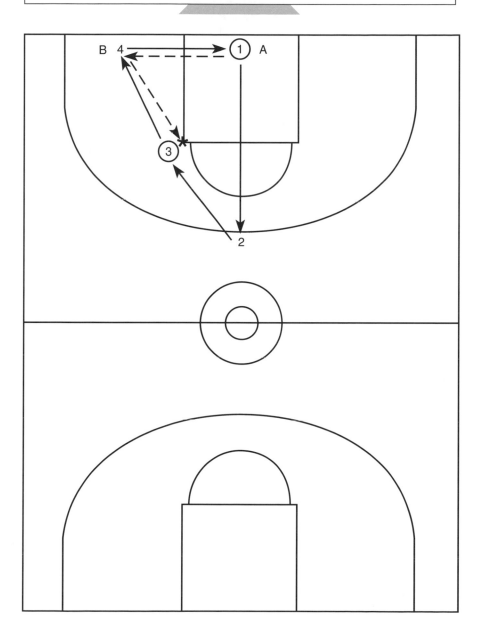

INDIVIDUAL 22

(1) Start—shoot five jumpers from the three-point line or the top of the key

1-2 Sprint

2-3 Sprint—receive pass at the three-point line or the top of the key

(3) Four jumpers

3-4 Sprint

4-5 Sprint—receive pass at the three-point line or the top of the key

(5) Three jumpers

5-6 Sprint

6-7 Sprint—receive pass at the three-point line or the top of the key

(7) Two jumpers

7-8 Sprint

8-9 Sprint—receive pass at the three-point line or the top of the key

(9) One jumper

Rotate passer to shooter, shooter to rebounder, rebounder to passer

Note: Use two basketballs.

*Rebounder passes to passer, passer passes to shooter.

Variations:

1. To make the drill more demanding, try "pyramid" shooting (shoot positions 5, 4, 3, 2, 1, 1, 2, 3, 4, 5). Follow sprint routine (described above) between each set of shots.

2. For a faster-paced drill, sprint to half-court only.

3. Vary the shooting spots (elbow, top of the key, baseline corner, etc.).

4. Have the players perform three to five rim/backboard taps at the opposite basket during the sprint phase.

5. If dealing with larger numbers of players, assign six players per half-court (two groups of three players). During the sprint phase, the players run to the baseline corner instead of under the opposite basket. Players must communicate to avoid collision. Rotate shooter to rebounder, rebounder to passer, passer to shooter.

INDIVIDUAL 22

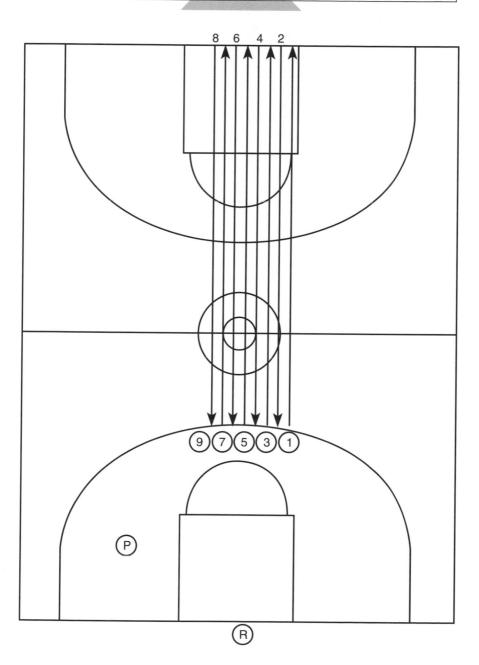

INDIVIDUAL 23

(A1) Start at the baseline corner

(B1) Start under the basket

(C1) Start at the baseline corner opposite player A

All three players start simultaneously
Player B passes to player C at ★
Player C passes back to player B at ★
Player B passes to player A at ★

(A2) Power lay-up

(B2) Touch baseline corner with foot (player B cuts behind player A after the pass)

(C2) Rebound

(A3), (B3), and (C3) Repeat in the opposite direction

Player C passes to player A
Player A passes back to player C
Player C passes to player B
This time player B executes the lay-up and player A rebounds
Continue the pattern for several repetitions

Variation:

When dealing with large numbers of players (six or more), arrange group 1 at one end of the court and group 2 at the opposite end. If you have nine players, then group 3 would start at the same end as group 1. If you have 12 players, then group 4 would start at the same end as group 2, and so on. Group 1 will start and end at the same spot. As group 1 crosses half-court as they sprint their last weave (repetitions to be predetermined), group 2 starts. Likewise, group 2 will end where they started. On the last sprint, group 3 starts as group 2 crosses half-court. Repeat with subsequent groups or start over with group 1.

INDIVIDUAL 23

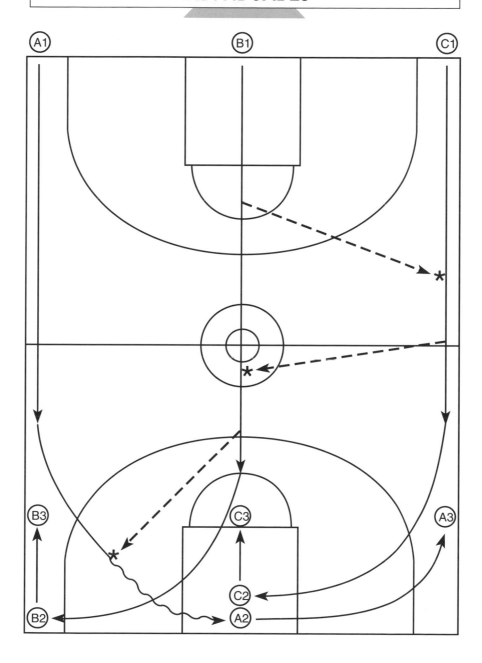

INDIVIDUAL 24

(A1) Start at the baseline corner

A1-A2 Back-pedal to half-court/sideline junction

A2-A3 Power shuffle to the circle

A3-A4 Sprint to the baseline

A4-A5 Sprint

(A5) Three rim/backboard taps

A5-A6 Sprint

(A6) The first player to arrive at center court picks up the ball and drives to the basket. The other player must catch up and defend.

A6-A7 Offense or defense to the basket

(A7) Score or turnover

   End

Variations:

1. Keep score, either by teams or individuals. Award one point for a "make," one point for a turnover.

2. Incorporate a second player, which will result in a two-on-two situation. Everything outlined above remains the same. However, player A's partner and player B's partner are standing at the elbow. When a player picks up the ball first, this player makes his or her team the offense. Score or turnover ends the game. Partners switch so that all players have the opportunity to run the drill pattern.

INDIVIDUAL 24

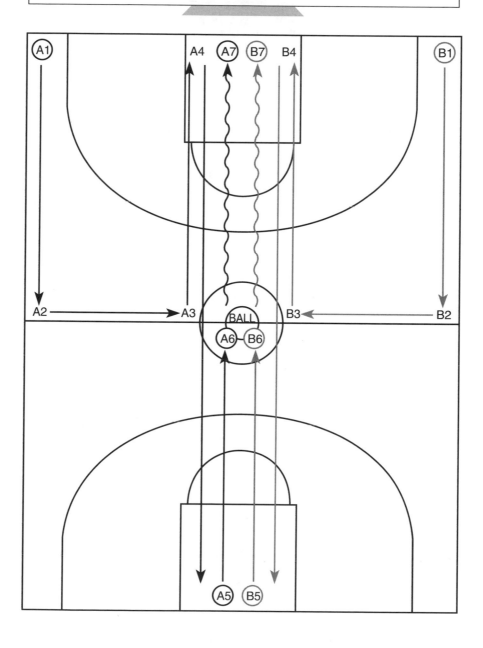

INDIVIDUAL 25

(P)   Passer is at center court with one or two balls

(1)   Start under the basket—perform three rim/backboard taps

1-2   Power shuffle—facing the near baseline

2-3   Power shuffle—facing the near baseline

(3)   Three rim/backboard taps

3-4   Back-pedal

4-5   Sprint

(5)   Three rim/backboard taps

5-6   Power shuffle—facing the near baseline

6-7   Power shuffle—facing the near baseline

(7)   Three rim/backboard taps

7-8   Sprint

8-9   Sprint—receive pass at ★, drive to the basket

(9)   Dunk/power lay-up

9-10   Sprint

10-11 Sprint—receive pass at ★, drive to the basket

(11)   Dunk/power lay-up

       End or repeat pattern in the opposite direction

Note: Rebounder passes to passer, passer passes to shooter.

Variations:

1. The player can shoot a jumper instead of performing the dunk/power lay-up. After shooting the jumper, the player must still follow the shot, touch the baseline, and then continue with the above pattern.

2. Several players can perform this drill simultaneously. Eliminate the rim/backboard taps, stagger the start, and make sure the players communicate to avoid collision.
   Note: Player B starts when player A gets to position 6.

3. Add a back shuffle/defensive slide to the drill. The player moves from position 1 to 2 and from position 2 to 3 while continuing to power shuffle, but then back shuffles/defensive slides to the three-point line at a 45° angle to the basket. The player sprints back to the basket and performs three rim/backboard taps. Next, the player should back-pedal to position 4, and so on.

4. Have the coach (rebounder/passer) point the direction of movement. For example, when the coach points toward the sideline, the player power shuffles in that direction. When the coach slaps the

INDIVIDUAL 25

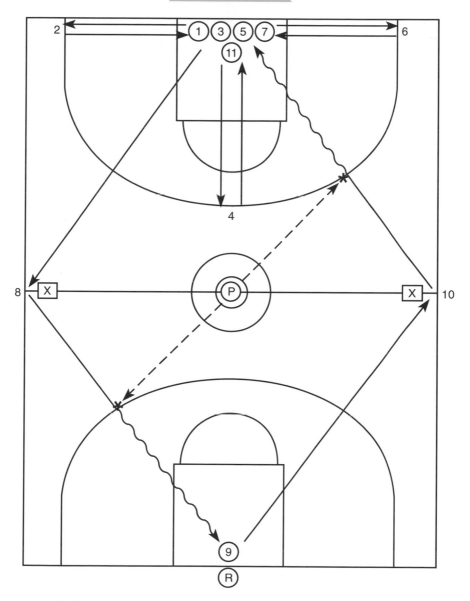

ball, the player sprints back to the basket and performs three rim/
backboard taps, then looks to the coach for the next directional
signal. After 30 seconds or so, the coach shouts "Go!" The player
sprints the above-described pattern (i.e., from position 7 to 8, from
position 8 to 9, from position 9 to 10, and from position 10 to 11).

CHAPTER 9

TEAM DRILLS

The drills illustrated in this section

work great for large numbers of players such as entire teams. Many of them, however, can be used by individuals, pairs, and small groups of players. Any time large numbers of players are participating at a high intensity, good communication is essential to avoid congestion and injury.

Have your drills planned out in advance of the training session. Keep in mind the purpose of that day's workouts. Is the emphasis on technique or conditioning? If conditioning, then what energy system is the focus? Also, always allow for adequate recovery between exercises, sets of exercises, and training sessions.

Team drills involve more game-like conditions than the individual drills because you have to consider not only your own position on the court, but also the positions of your teammates and opponents. Developing this "court sense" is *almost* as important as developing your body.

TEAM 1

(1) Start on the baseline

1-2 Sprint

2-3 Sprint

3-4 Sprint

4-5 Sprint

5-6 Sprint

6-7 Sprint

(7) Continue for a predetermined number of round trips

Note: All of group 1 players complete the drill before group 2 begins.
*Depending on the energy system being trained, typically rest for group 1 is limited to the time required for groups 2 and 3 to complete the drill.
*Must touch baselines and half-court line with foot.

Variations:

1. This drill can be done while dribbling a ball.

2. Follow this procedure to make the drill more demanding: When a player arrives at a baseline, instead of touching the line with the foot, the player drops and performs five push-ups. For example, start with five push-ups at position 1. Sprint from position 1 to 2 (the opposite baseline) and do five more push-ups. Continue the routine, performing push-ups every time the athlete arrives at a baseline (positions 1, 2, 4, 5, and 7).

TEAM 1

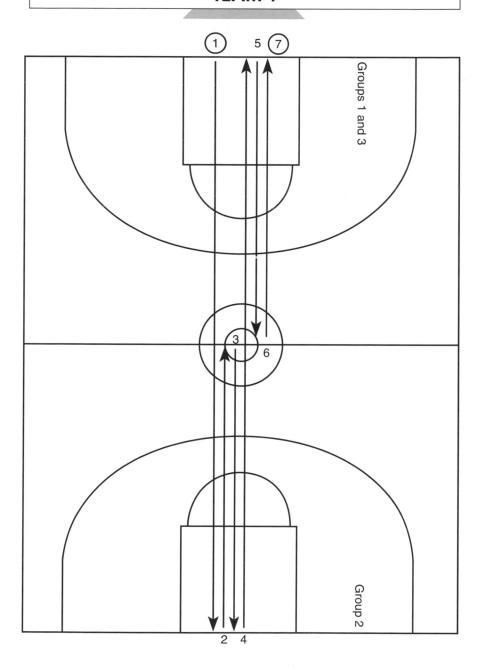

TEAM 2

Many times in a competitive situation, an athlete may lose his or her balance or get knocked to the floor. If the athlete is uninjured, rapidly regaining control and rejoining teammates will contribute much more to the team than remaining on the floor or complaining to the referee. "Get-ups" are drills that train the athlete in this quick response. Players begin in an awkward position and then, on command (whistle, "Go!," clap, etc.), immediately regain body control and explosively accelerate into a sprint. The beginning positions listed here are only samples. Use your creativity to add to the repertoire. Players should concentrate on a quick response to the auditory signal and an explosive acceleration.

(1)   Start on the baseline—"Get-up" drill—coach's choice

1-2   Accelerate/sprint

2-3   Jog

(3)   Repeat in the opposite direction—"Get-up" drill—coach's choice

Options for starting positions:
1. Hands and knees facing direction of sprint
2. Hands and knees facing away from direction of sprint
3. Seated with legs straight facing direction of sprint
4. Seated with legs straight facing away from direction of sprint
5. Prone facing direction of sprint
6. Prone facing away from direction of sprint
7. Supine facing direction of sprint
8. Supine facing away from direction of sprint

Note: When the athlete is facing *away* from the direction of the sprint, he or she must *quickly* turn and accelerate/sprint.

Variations:
1. The team is divided into groups of three. Each group lines up on the baseline with the player at the head of each line positioned in one of the starting positions listed above. The ball is placed at center court. On the coach's command, all three players get up and sprint to the ball. The first player to pick up the ball drives to the opposite basket. The other two players chase and defend.
2. Same drill as above but four players are involved (two teams of two players). When a player picks up the ball, this player's team is on offense, with the other team of two defending.

TEAM 2

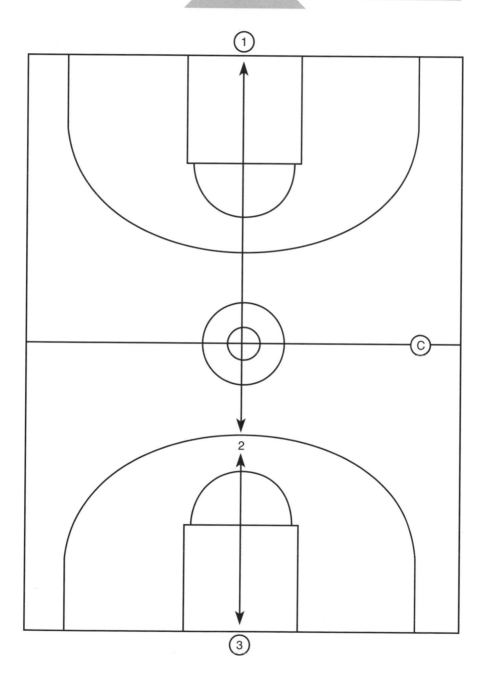

TEAM 3

(1) Start under the basket

1-2 Sprint

2-3 Power shuffle or carioca

3-4 Back-pedal, back run, or back shuffle/defensive slide

4-5 Power shuffle or carioca

(5) Repeat

Note: Maintain even spacing between players.

Variations:

1. For movement from position 1 to 2, incorporate skipping, high-knee running, running with hands above head, and so on.

2. Have players dribble a ball while running the pattern.

TEAM 3

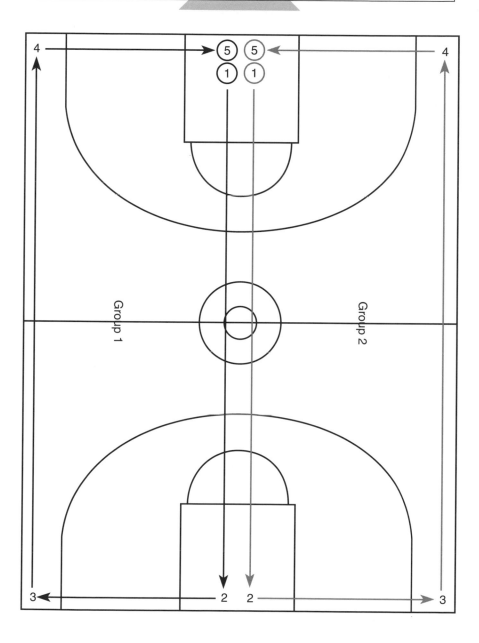

TEAM 4

(1)   Start on the baseline

1-2   Sprint

(2)   Hand on the floor—run clockwise

2-3   Sprint

(3)   Hand on the floor—run counterclockwise

3-4   Sprint

(4)   Hand on the floor—run clockwise

4-5   Sprint

(5)   Hand on the floor—run counterclockwise

5-6   Sprint

6-7   Power shuffle

7-8   Back-pedal or quick jog

8-9   Power shuffle

(9)   Repeat

Note: When first player crosses the near free-throw line, the next player starts. Maintain even spacing.

Variation:

This drill can be done as a timed sprint from position 1 to 6. Jog back to position 1 and do several repetitions per set.

TEAM 4

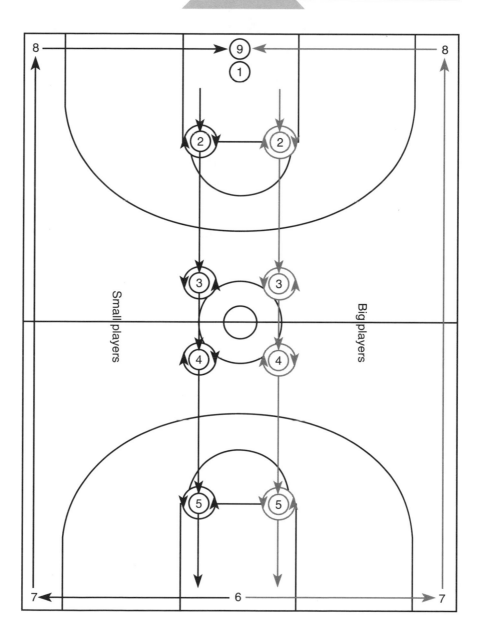

TEAM 5

(1)   Start—quick jumps *forward and back* over the baseline

1-2   Sprint on coach's command (clap, "Go!", whistle, etc.)

(2)   Quick jumps *side to side* over the half-court line

2-3   Sprint on coach's command

(3)   End group 1, start group 2 in opposite direction

Note: All of group 1 players complete the drill before group 2 begins.
   *Depending on the energy system being trained, typically rest for group 1 is limited to the time required for groups 2 and 3 to complete the drill.
   *Repeat for a set time or a predetermined number of repetitions.

Variations:

1. To increase the demand on the quick jumps, have the athlete jump over a small barrier (rolled up towel, foam, etc.).

2. Incorporate various movement patterns, such as high-knee running, power shuffle, back-pedal, and back shuffle/defensive slide between quick jumps.

TEAM 5

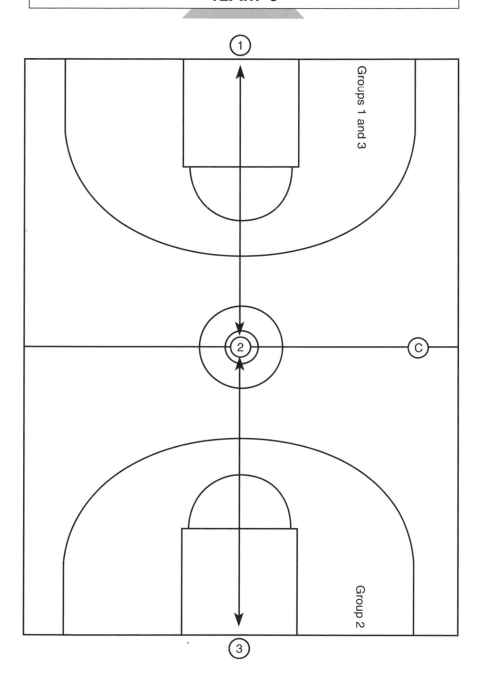

TEAM 6

Player A tries to cross the free-throw line

Player B tries to prevent player A from crossing the line by "hand checking"

Player A cannot force himself or herself across the line

Player A can sprint, shuffle, pivot, fake, or do whatever it takes to cross the line untouched

If player A crosses the line untouched, he or she quickly moves around the nearest cone and the drill continues until the predetermined time has expired

Rest

Switch—player B is on offense, player A is on defense

Note: Start with 30-second work intervals. As conditioning levels rise, increase work time.

Variation:

This drill can be done as a competition. Record each player's number of successful crosses during the predetermined work interval. Allow for a full recovery, then have players switch from offense to defense and vice versa.

TEAM 6

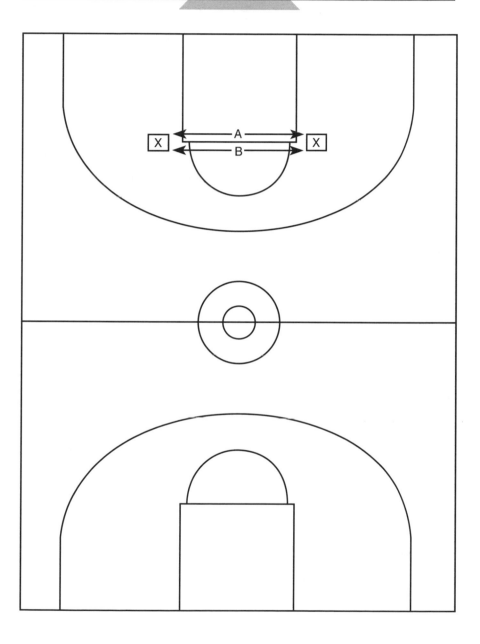

TEAM 7

1-2 Sprint

2-3 Power shuffle

3-4 Back-pedal

4-1 Power shuffle

On coach's command, players A, B, C, and D start

Each player tries to catch the player ahead

When the player ahead is tagged, he or she drops out

Race continues until only one player remains

Note: Players always face the same direction.
*Cones are placed 5 to 15 yards apart.
*Players must cut *outside* of the cones.
*If only two players are participating, start at positions 1 and 3.

Variation:

Try sprinting and dribbling around the square. Perform this drill both clockwise (left-hand dribble) and counterclockwise (right-hand dribble).

TEAM 7

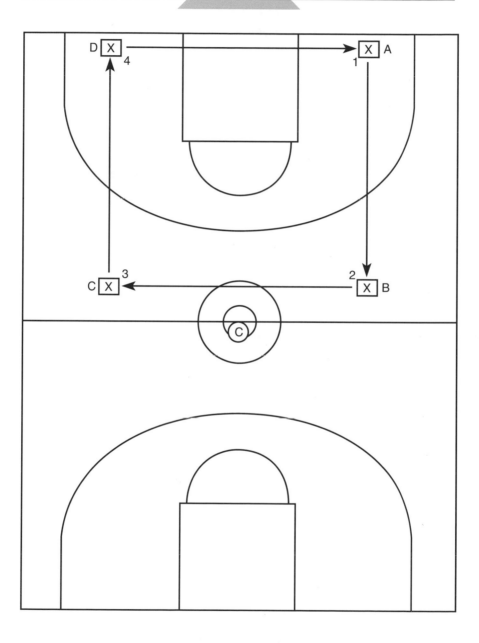

TEAM 8

(1)　Group 1 starts on the baseline

1-2　Sprint

2-3　Sprint

3-4　Sprint

4-5　Sprint

5-6　Sprint

6-7　Sprint

7-8　Sprint

(8)　End group 1, start group 2 in the opposite direction

Note: All of group 1 players complete the drill before group 2 begins.
  *Depending on the energy system being trained, typically rest for group 1 is limited to the time required for groups 2 and 3 to complete the drill.
  *Repeat for a predetermined number of repetitions or a set time.

Variations:

1. Incorporate a variety of movement patterns into the drill (power shuffle, back-pedal, back shuffle/defensive slide, high-knee running, skipping, etc.). Always sprint to the finish (from position 7 to 8).

2. Make the transition more demanding by requiring the players to touch the floor with the hand at the "turn-around" point.

TEAM 8

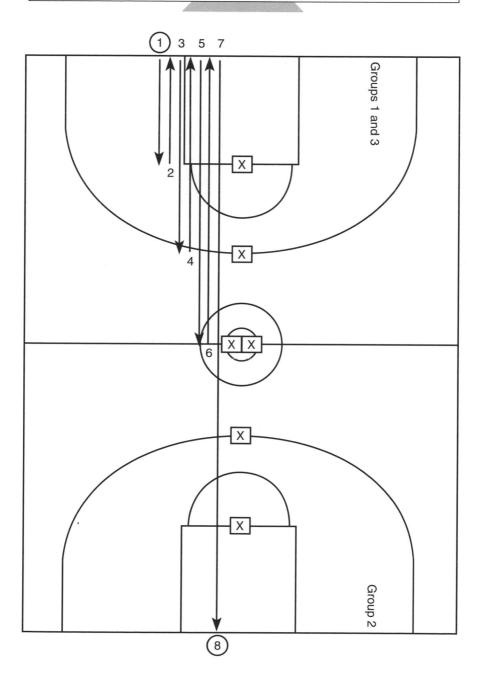

TEAM 9

(1)   Start

1-2   Sprint, weaving in and out of the cones

2-3   Jog or power shuffle

3-4   Back-pedal or back shuffle/defensive slide *carefully* weaving in and out of the cones

4-5   Jog or power shuffle

(5)   Repeat

Note: When the first player crosses the near free-throw line, the next player starts.
   *Cones are spaced 5 yards apart—number of cones may vary.
   *Quick transition *around* cones.
   *Maintain even spacing between players.

Variations:

1. To enhance agility have the player bend at the knees and touch the top of each cone as he or she passes. The player should focus on maintaining speed while touching the cones.

2. Incorporate dribbling a basketball.

TEAM 9

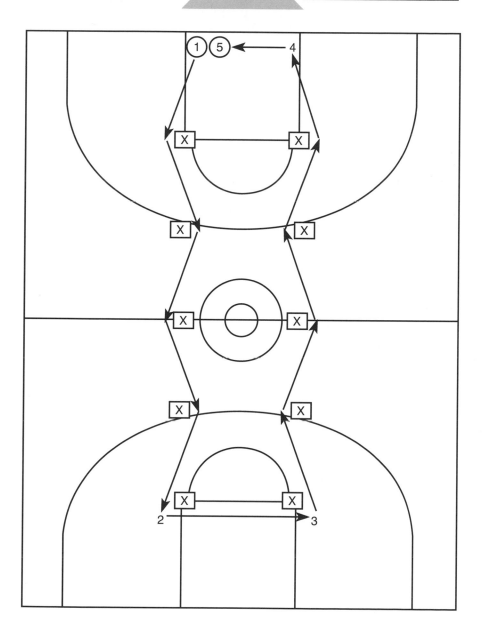

TEAM 10

(1) Start

1-2 Sprint

2-3 Power shuffle

3-4 Sprint

4-5 Power shuffle

5-6 Sprint

6-7 Power shuffle

7-8 Sprint

8-9 Power shuffle

9-10 Jog

10-11 Jog

11-12 Jog

(12) Repeat

Note: When the first player reaches position 2, the next player starts.
   *Cones are spaced 5 yards apart—the number of cones may vary.
   *Quick transition *around* cones.
   *Maintain even spacing between players.

Variation:

For a more advanced drill, follow the same routine outlined above but try back shuffling/defensive sliding or back-pedaling in place of sprinting (note: power shuffle remains the same).

TEAM 10

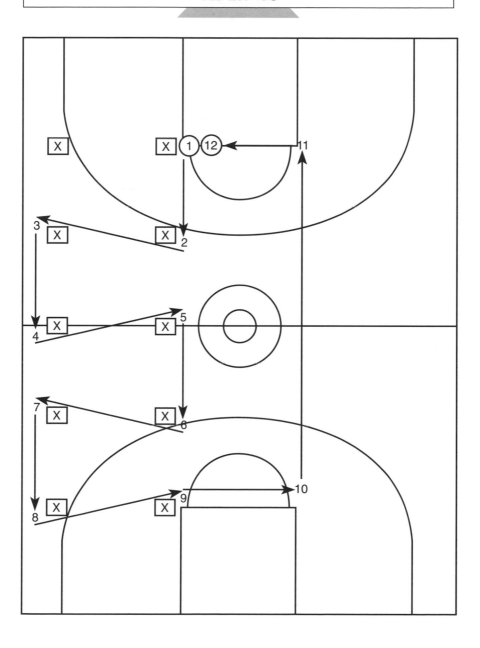

TEAM 11

(1) Start

1-2 Sprint

2-3 Power shuffle

3-4 Sprint

4-5 Power shuffle

5-6 Sprint

6-7 Power shuffle

7-8 Sprint

8-9 Power shuffle

9-10 Jog

10-11 Jog

11-12 Jog

(12) Repeat pattern in opposite direction (position 12 to 3 sprint, 3 to 2 power shuffle, 2 to 5 sprint, 5 to 4 power shuffle, etc.)

Note: When the first player reaches cone 2, the next player starts.
   *Cones are spaced 5 yards apart—number of cones may vary.
   *Quick transition *around* cones.
   *Maintain even spacing between players.

Variation:

Once the players are comfortable with the above drill pattern, divide the team into two groups. Group A is lined up behind cone 1. Group B is lined up behind cone 12. The first player in each group begins by power shuffling diagonally *around* the next cone (instead of sprinting as outlined above). For example, group A's player 1 power shuffles from position 1 to 2, cuts *around* cone 2, and power shuffles from position 2 to 3, position 3 to 4, and so on. Group B's player 1 performs the same routine but starts at position 12 and power shuffles to cone 3, cuts *around* cone 3, and power shuffles from position 3 to 2, position 2 to 5, and so on. After player 1 finishes, he or she jogs back to the opposite "start" cone. The coach can either stagger the start to lessen the congestion on the crossover, or have the players start simultaneously and therefore, intentionally cause congestion at the crossover. In this case, the players must work as a team and communicate to avoid collision.

TEAM 11

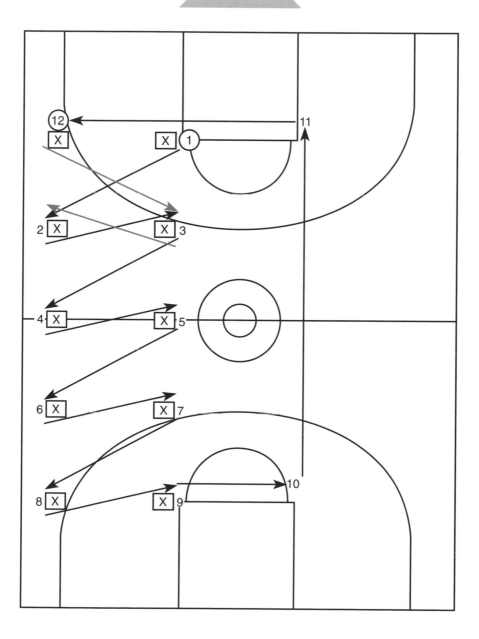

TEAM 12

(1)   Start with six players standing in the center circle, each facing a different cone

1-2   Sprint

(2)   Touch cone

2-3   Sprint

3-4   Sprint

(4)   Touch cone

4-5   Sprint

5-6   Sprint

(6)   Touch cone

6-7   Sprint

7-8   Sprint

(8)   Touch cone

8-9   Sprint

9-10 Sprint

(10) Touch cone

10-11 Sprint

11-12 Sprint

(12) Touch cone

12-1 Sprint

(1)   End or repeat

Note: Can be performed as an individual or a team drill.
   *Initially, start with six cones. As proficiency improves, increase to 8, 10, and then 12 cones.

Variations:

1. Incorporate a variety of movement patterns, such as power shuffle, high-knee running, skipping, and so on. For example, back-pedal from the center circle to the cone. Always sprint back to the circle.

TEAM 12

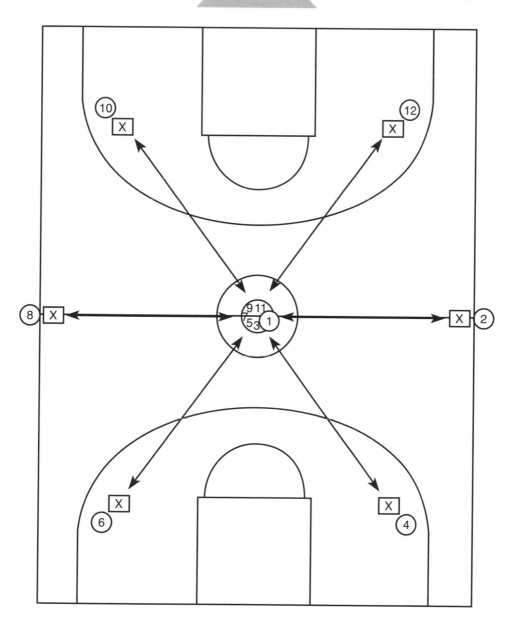

2. For a demanding competition, try playing tag (catch the player ahead). Use six cones but only three players. The game ends either when one player is tagged, or when only one player remains. To speed the game up, move the cones closer to the center circle.

TEAM 13

(1)   Start at the baseline corner

1-2   Sprint to the center circle

2-3   Reverse pivot and power shuffle facing the near baseline

3-4   Reverse pivot and back-pedal—communicate during the cross-over to avoid collision

4-5   Power shuffle facing the far baseline

(5)   Repeat

Note: Maintain even spacing between players—communicate during the crossover.

Variations:

1. From position 1 to 2, incorporate skipping, high-knee running, running with hands above head, and so on.

2. Incorporate dribbling a ball.

3. This drill is a great conditioner. It can be performed with one group using the full court or two to four small groups as illustrated.

TEAM 13

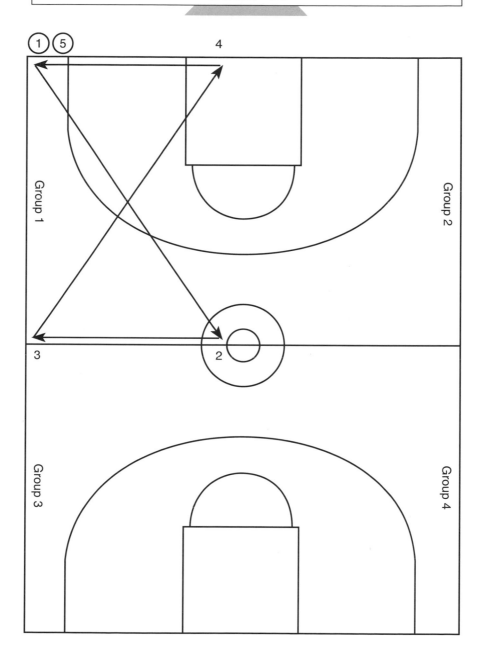

TEAM 14

(1)   Start under the basket with a partner

1-2   Power shuffle facing partner

(2)   Step back 2 to 3 feet

2-3   Power shuffle, still facing partner

(3)   Reverse pivot

3-4   Power shuffle

(4)   Step back 2 to 3 feet

4-5   Power shuffle

(5)   Reverse pivot

5-6   Power shuffle

6-7   Jog

(7)   Face partner—repeat on the opposite side

Note: When first player crosses the free-throw line, the next player starts.
*Group 2 mirrors group 1.
*Players must communicate to avoid collision.

Variation:

As proficiency improves, confine the drill to just the free-throw lane (see the diagrammed short version).

TEAM 14

Long version

Short version

TEAM 15

(1)   Start at the three-point line (or sideline)

1-2   Power shuffle facing the near baseline

(2)   Reverse pivot to face the coach/passer

2-3   Coach/passer passes the ball; player performs a dunk/power lay-up, rebounds own ball, and passes back to coach/passer

(3)   Reverse pivot to face the near baseline

3-4   Power shuffle

(4)   Repeat—opposite direction

Note: Each set should last 30 seconds to 2 minutes.

Variations:

1. Eliminate steps 2 and 3 in the above description. The player power shuffles facing the near baseline from position 1 to 4. On coach's command, "turn," the player pivots and receives a pass from the coach/passer. The player then spins, drives to the basket, performs a dunk/power lay-up, rebounds the ball, passes back to the coach/ passer, faces the near baseline, and continues shuffling.

2. The entire team can perform this drill simultaneously (spaced evenly over the court). Eliminate the pass and dunk/power lay-up. Cones may need to be placed through the center of the court to help players recognize pivot spots.

TEAM 15

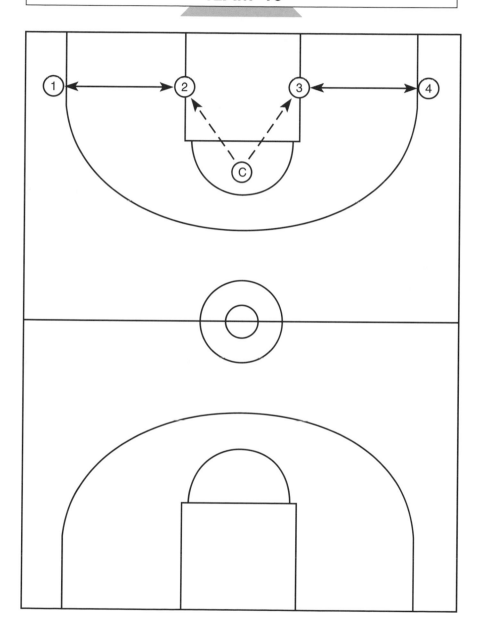

TEAM 16

(A1)   Player A is positioned 10 to 15 feet away from and facing player B

Both players A and B are holding a ball

To start, player A passes to player C while simultaneously receiving a pass from player B

A1-A2   Power shuffle—player A continues to pass to the next player ahead while receiving the ball from the previous player

(A2)   When player A arrives at position A2, player F hesitates passing the ball until player A starts reversing direction by passing ahead to player E.

A2-A3   Power shuffle and pass

A3-A4   Power shuffle and pass

Continue the pattern for several repetitions. Always end on the opposite end of the start

(A4)   End for player A

Player A moves to player F's position and all players shift right

Player B steps up and assumes player A's position

Variation:

Try varying the passes. Either be consistent with the passes (i.e., all chest, all bounce, etc.) through the duration of the drills, or have the passers (players B, C, D, E, and F) dictate the passes. For example, player A receives a pass and executes the same kind of pass to the next player in line.

TEAM 16

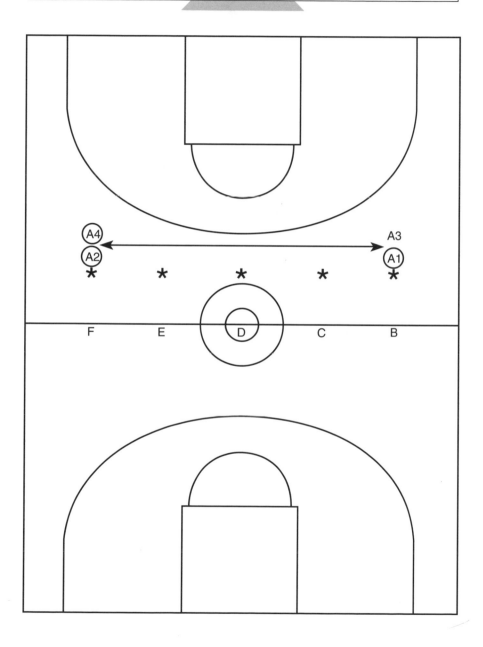

TEAM 17

(1)   Start

1-2   Player A is on offense and dribbling; player B is defending player A, back shuffling/defensive sliding with pivot

2-3   Quick jog

(3)   Switch

3-4   Player B is on offense and dribbling; player A is defending player B, back shuffling/defensive sliding with pivot

4-5   Quick jog

(5)   Switch

Repeat

Note: Next pair starts as first pair crosses X.
   *Drill is performed for 1 to 5 minutes.
   *Quick pivots.
   *Control the ball—defender applies pressure but does not disrupt the dribble.
   *Maintain even spacing.

Variation:

Offensive players can either face forward, face backward, or combine positions when bringing the ball up court.

TEAM 17

TEAM 18

① Start by tipping the ball against the backboard

1-2 Players are evenly spaced, each taking turns to tip the ball *once* against the backboard (the ball should not hit floor)

Players sprint around coach and back to the basket to continue the "tip" drill

Variations:

1. As the team gains confidence and conditioning levels improve, the coach gradually moves further back, thus requiring the players to run further and, ultimately, faster.

2. For a team competition, place one cone at center court and divide the team into two equal groups, one group per basket. At their respective baskets, have both groups follow the directions outlined above. After the tip, have each player sprint around the center-court cone. Players must communicate to avoid collision. Both groups must circle the cone on the same side, either clockwise or counterclockwise. Note: This drill works best with a large number of participants.

TEAM 18

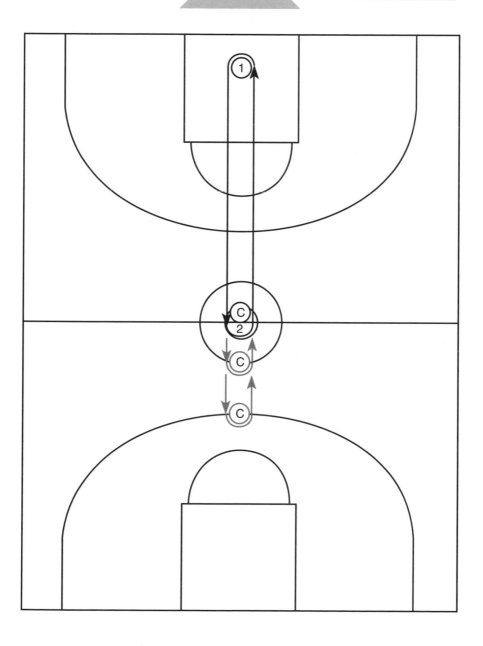

TEAM 19

(1)   Start with players dribbling a ball

1-2   Sprint

2-3   Power shuffle

3-4   Sprint

4-5   Power shuffle

5-6   Sprint

(6)   Lay-up (player rebounds own ball)

6-7   Jog

(7)   Start

7-8   Sprint

8-9   Power shuffle

9-10 Sprint

10-11 Power shuffle

11-12 Sprint

(12) Lay-up (player rebounds own ball)

12-13 Jog

(13) Continue for several round trips, then repeat the pattern in the opposite direction

Note: When the first player reaches position 2, the next player starts.
  *For large numbers of players, start half of them at position 1 and the other half at position 7.

Variations:

1. This drill can be performed with or without a ball. Players should jump and touch the backboard instead of doing a lay-up.

2. Incorporate various movement patterns such as high-knee running, skipping, back-pedaling, and back shuffle/defensive slide, from position 1 to 2, position 3 to 4, position 7 to 8, and position 9 to 10. Power shuffle or carioca from position 2 to 3, position 4 to 5, position 8 to 9, and position 10 to 11. Always sprint from position 5 to 6 and position 11 to 12.

TEAM 19

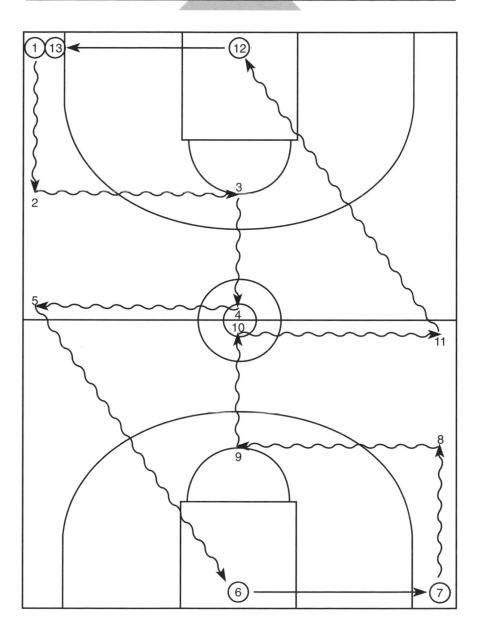

TEAM 20

(A1) and (B1) Start

A1-A2 Sprint—player A dribbling

B1-B2 Sprint—player B

(A2) Jump stop, reverse pivot—player A passes to player B at ★

(B2) Player B receives pass from player A at the elbow

A2-A3 Sprint—player A sprints to the basket but does not interfere with player B's lay-up

B2-B3 Player B drives to the basket

(B3) Power lay-up—player B

(A3) Player A rebounds the ball and passes an outlet to player B who is sprinting toward position B4

A3-A4 Sprint—player A

B3-B4 Sprint—player B

(B4) Player B passes the ball ahead to the next player in line who has started sprinting toward position A2

A4-A5 Sprint—player A

B4-B5 Sprint—player B

(A5) Touch coach's hand and continue drill; player A becomes player B

(B5) Touch coach's hand and continue drill; player B becomes player A

Note: The next player in line starts as player A reaches the pivot spot.
   *Use two or three balls.
   *Maintain even spacing between players.
   *There should be no stopping or standing in line.
   *Continue for a predetermined number of repetitions or a set time, then repeat on the opposite side.

Variations:

1. Coaches can vary the distance of the run (they can stand at half-court, the three-point line, or on the opposite baseline).

2. For large numbers of players, divide the team into two groups. Use two baskets, but only run to half-court.

TEAM 20

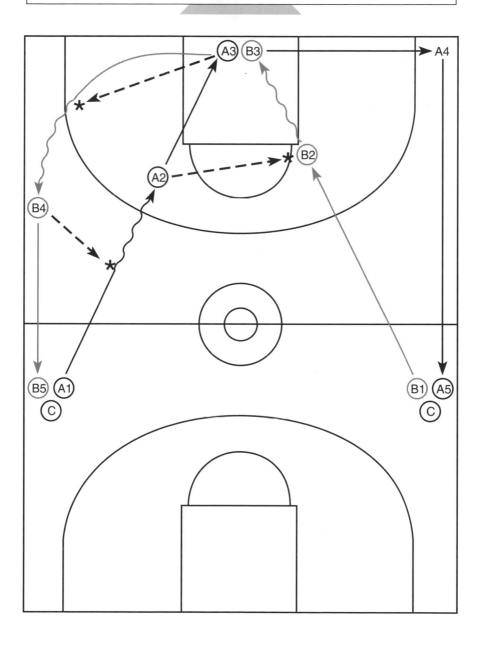

TEAM 21

(A1) and (B1) Start at the half-court/sideline junction

A1-A2 Sprint—player A dribbling

B1-B2 Sprint—player B

(A2)   Power lay-up—player A

(B2)   Rebound—player B

A2-A3 Player A is on defense—back shuffle/defensive slide

B2-B3 Player B is on offense—dribbling

A3-A4 Power shuffle—player A

B3-B4 Power shuffle—player B

A4-A5 Sprint—player A

B4-B5 Sprint—player B

(A5)   Repeat; player A becomes player B

(B5)   Repeat; player B becomes player A

Note: The next pair starts after first pair rebounds the ball.
    *Each pair has a ball.
    *Maintain even spacing between players.
    *Continuous running, no stopping.

Variation:

For a faster-paced drill, divide the team into two groups (one group per half-court). Run the same pattern described above using half the court. It is helpful to place a cone midway between the baseline and the half-court line to indicate positions A1 and B1.

TEAM 21

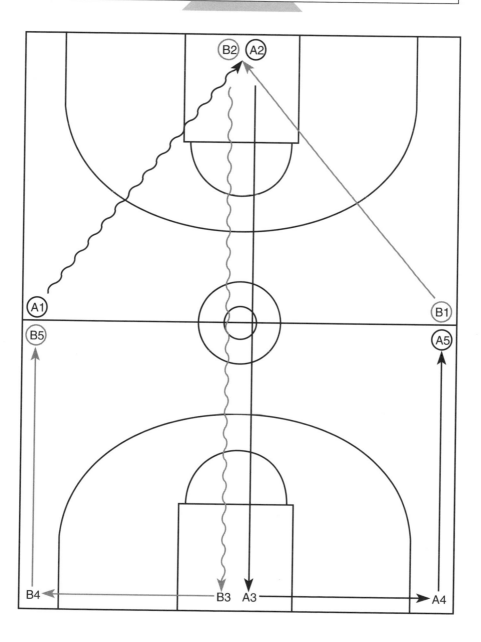

TEAM 22

Player A passes to player B and follows the pass

Player B passes back to player A

Player A spins and dunks or makes a power lay-up

Player A gets his or her own rebound, passes to player C, and follows the pass

Player C passes back to player A

Player A spins and dunks or makes a power lay-up

Player A gets his or her own rebound, passes to player B, and follows the pass

Repeat the pattern

Note: On coach's command or after a set number of made baskets, players rotate (A to B, B to C, C to A).
*After all players complete their turns, switch to the other side of the basket.
*Make sure players communicate to avoid a collision with teammates working on the opposite side of the basket.

Variations:

1. Player A passes to player B and follows the pass, but instead of receiving a pass back from player B, player A defends one-on-one as player B drives to the basket. After player B's shot or turnover, player A immediately retrieves the ball and passes to player C and repeats. Meanwhile, player B returns to his or her starting position. The drill continues for a predetermined number of repetitions or a set time and then players rotate.

Note: This variation should only be performed with one group of three players per basket.

2. This works well as an individual drill. The coach or another player shifts from position B to C, playing both spots.

TEAM 22

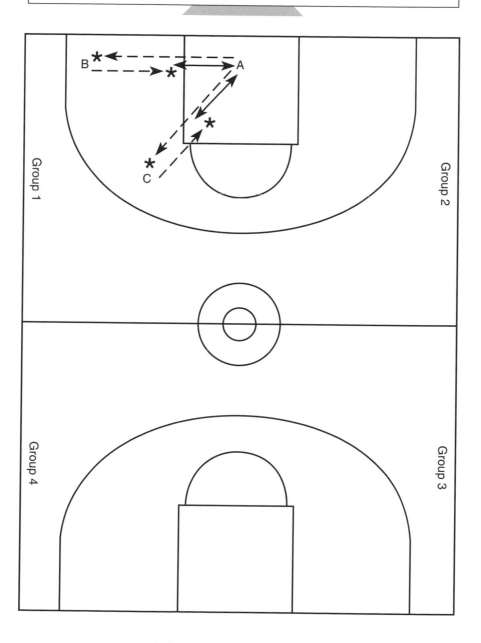

TEAM 23

(1)　Start—player A shoots a jumper

1-2　Player A sprints to the basket

(2)　Player A rebounds own shot and passes to player B at position 3

2-3　Player A follows the pass, sprinting

(3)　Player B passes to player C, who is sprinting from position 4 to position 5

3-4　Sprint—player B

4-5　Sprint—player C

(5)　Player C receives pass from player B and shoots a jumper

Continue the pattern

Note: On coach's command or a set number of made baskets, players should work the opposite side of the basket.

Variations:

1. Vary the shooting spots (three-point line, top of the key, free-throw line, etc.).

2. For competition, the first team to hit a predetermined number of shots (15 to 30) wins.

3. Incorporate other movement patterns (power shuffle, back shuffle/ defensive slide, back-pedal, etc.) between positions.

TEAM 23

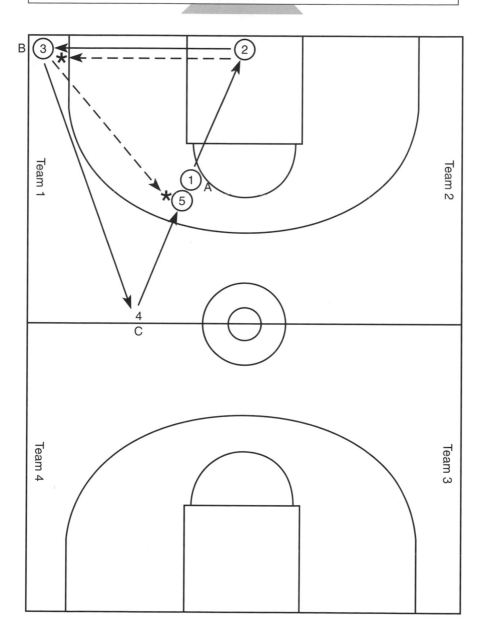

TEAM 24

① Start—receive pass from rebounder and shoot a jumper from deep baseline corner

1-2 Sprint

2-3 Sprint—receive pass from rebounder at the top of the key

③ Jumper

3-4 Sprint

4-5 Sprint

5-6 Back-pedal

6-7 Sprint—receive pass from rebounder at the top of the key

⑦ Jumper

7-8 Sprint

8-9 Sprint—receive pass from rebounder as approaching the baseline corner

⑨ Jumper

If single runner, continue in opposite direction

If entire team is participating, wait until all players have completed one repetition, then repeat in the opposite direction, or jog to position 1 and start the pattern again

Variations:
1. The entire team can perform this drill, but the start must be staggered (as the first player crosses half-court, the next player in line starts). Even spacing should be maintained throughout.

Note: Several rebounder/passers are required.

2. Divide the team into two groups and run the same pattern using half the court.

TEAM 24

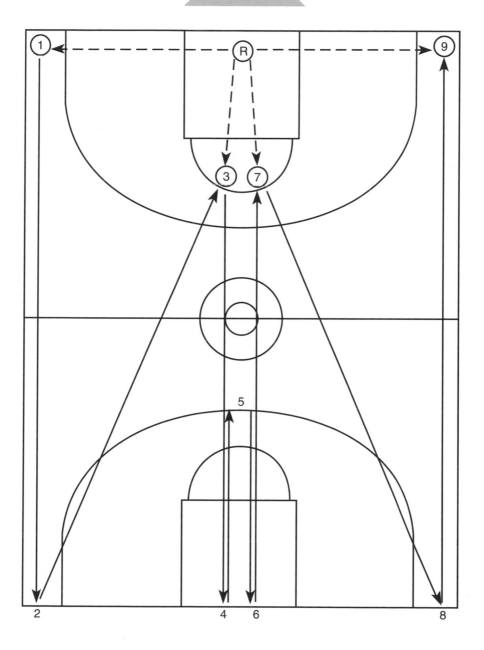

TEAM 25

(1)   Start—player A receives pass from player B (the rebounder) and shoots a jumper

1-X1   Sprint—player A

X1-X2-X1 Low defensive stance—player A guards player C (Both players power shuffle one to five round trips between cones or player A power shuffles and mirrors player C; player C can shuffle, sprint, pivot, or whatever it takes to "lose" player A; on the coach's command, player A sprints to the next shooting spot)

X1-2   Sprint—player A receives pass from player B

(2)   Jumper—player A

2-X1   Sprint—player A

X1-X2-X1 Low defensive stance—player A guards player C

X1-3   Sprint—player A receives pass from player B

(3)   Jumper—player A

3-X1   Sprint—player A

X1-X2-X1 Low defensive stance—player A guards player C

Continue pattern (from position 1 to 5 and 5 back to 1 equals one set)

Rotate players (A to B, B to C, and C to A)

Note: In the above description, cones are used to indicate start and stop points (X1 and X2) but are not necessary when actually performing the drill.

*Two groups at each basket; work both sides of the floor.

Variations:

1. Player B throws an outlet pass to player C. Player A sprints to defend player C (defensive shuffle X1 to X2). On the coach's command, player A is allowed to steal the ball and sprints to the next shooting spot. Continue pattern from positions 1 through 5 and positions 5 through 1.

2. Player B passes to player A, then steps up to defend player A's jumper. While player A sprints and touches player C's hand, player B rebounds the ball and prepares to defend player A's next shot.

TEAM 25

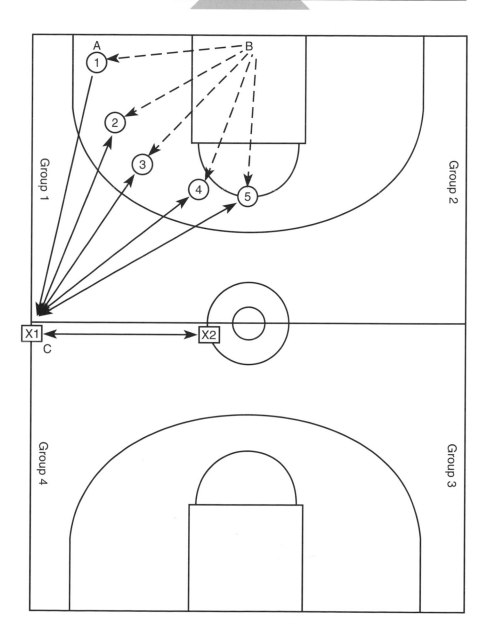

CHAPTER 10

BASKETBALL CONDITIONING PROGRAMS

Basketball conditioning would be much less complicated if a single training regimen could address all of the components of fitness and athleticism simultaneously. Unfortunately, no such conditioning program exists. As a result, it's essential that your training efforts emphasize the specific physical needs required to play basketball successfully.

Some players mistakenly think that playing a lot of games is all they need to get and stay in shape. Simply playing the game will not adequately challenge the physical requirements necessary to elevate specific basketball skills to a higher level. In addition to the components of fitness and athletic performance, a basketball player must adopt the total training philosophy that includes all of the previously mentioned athletic variables.

What you emphasize in your training can be largely determined by individual needs established through various assessment tools (see chapter 6). The test results will help you develop an individual assessment profile. Only after analyzing your test results and combining the observations and suggestions of your coach with the principles of fitness (chapter 1) and athleticism (chapter 5), can you develop a conditioning program that will produce an optimal training effect for basketball performance.

SAFETY CONSIDERATIONS

Before implementing any conditioning program, make sure you are aiming for the greatest physical benefits while minimizing unsafe circumstances that might lead to injuries. This is typically the responsibility of the coach, but players also need to do their part and use common sense.

Here are some general safety measures to follow during a training program:

- Always warm up and stretch prior to training, and always cool down after the session.
- Keep the basketball floor clean and free from obstructions.
- Wear shoes that provide proper lateral stability, sufficient heel cushion, and good arch support. Cross-trainers and basketball shoes work best.
- If large numbers of players are involved in the drill, communicate effectively to help avoid collisions.
- Although not entirely necessary, equipment such as cones and shooting dots that indicate transition points and shooting positions on the floor help eliminate confusion and keep the "flow" moving smoothly.
- Each player responds uniquely to the same program. Allow for adequate rest and recovery, depending on *your* fitness and tolerance level.
- Replenish fluids on a frequent basis—*before* you start to get thirsty.

DEVELOPING A PROGRAM

The focus of the training session is determined by the purpose of the activity, which may be (a) to develop movement skills and techniques, or (b) to condition the energy systems. Other variables that influence the design of the overall program and individual workouts include the training phase (e.g., off-season, pre-season, in-season) and the sets and repetitions of the exercise.

When using the court conditioning drills in this book, the following general guidelines provide the tools necessary to organize your own training regimen.

SEASON-BY-SEASON CONDITIONING GUIDELINES

Off-Season

Focus: Predominately aerobic in the early off-season. As the pre-season approaches greater emphasis is placed on the anaerobic system.

Frequency: 2-3 times per week

Duration: Long (20-60 minutes)

Intensity: Low

Rest intervals: Little or no rest between sets*

Pre-Season

Focus: Predominately anaerobic, training the energy system specific to basketball

Frequency: 3-5 times per week

Duration: Dictated by the intensity, number of sets, and rest interval (i.e., the higher the intensity and duration, the longer the rest interval; sets will vary)

Intensity: Moderate to high

Rest intervals: Brief rest between sets. To keep things simple, use a 1:1 work-rest ratio. For example, if the drill lasts 2 minutes, the rest interval should be 2 minutes.

In-Season

Focus: Predominately technique; some anaerobic

Frequency: 1-2 times per week

Duration: Short; typically, each drill/set should not exceed 3 minutes

Intensity: High; maximal or near maximal effort

Rest intervals: Long between sets

Notes:

1. If the drill/set lasts 60 seconds or less, the work-rest ratio would be 1:3 to 1:2 (see Table 10.1, p. 227). For example, if the set lasts 15 seconds, the rest interval will be between 45-30 seconds.

2. If the drill/set lasts longer than 60 seconds, the work-rest ratio will be 1:2 to 1:1 (see Table 10.1, p. 227). For example, if the set lasts 150 seconds, the rest interval will be between 300-150 seconds.
   Usually, the longer the drill, the shorter the rest interval. Likewise, the higher the intensity, the longer the rest.

*A set is defined as a collection of repetitions performed consecutively without rest. For example, an athlete might perform three sets of three repetitions of Team Drill 1. Repetitions or "reps" are simply the number of times a drill is performed without rest within one set; there may be one or several repetitions of a drill pattern per set.

Note: Court drills being used 1 to 3 days per week doesn't mean that training ceases on the other days.

Table 10.1 Intensity, Rest, and Duration

Seasonal emphasis	Focus	Drill intensity	Work-rest ratio	Duration of session (including rest interval)
Off-Season	Aerobic	Low	Continuous: no significant rest interval	20-60 minutes
Pre-Season	Anaerobic	Mod. to high	Short recovery 1:1 work-rest ratio	10-40 minutes
In-Season	Technique	High	Full recovery If the drill lasts 1-60 sec, use a 1:3 to 1:2 work-rest ratio. If the drill lasts 60-180 sec, use a 1:2 to 1:1 work-rest ratio.	5-30 minutes

Assessing Effort

Accurately assessing drill intensity is always a challenge. Taking your pulse is the best method for determining both aerobic and anaerobic exertion (chapter 1). A more subjective measure is perceived exertion. As a general rule, the workload intensity for anaerobic training should be at a level of moderate to high discomfort. As your fitness level improves and you become more comfortable, the intensity should be increased.

The training load can be determined by manipulating reps and sets. Depending on the level of play, basketball has a work-rest ratio of approximately 1:1 to 1:3. Where the ratio falls in that range depends on the energy system being trained. For example, a drill lasting 1 minute with a 1 minute rest would be a 1:1 work-rest ratio and would be specific to training the anaerobic energy system involved in basketball.

When using the court drills to train the aerobic system (typically in the early off-season), you should allow for little or no rest between sets. In other words, one drill would lead immediately into the next. The intensity of the drill, however, would be low.

If the focus of training is to enhance technique, then you should arrange the repetitions and sets to include a longer rest interval to allow for **full recovery** (1:3 to 1:1 depending on the length of each individual drill/set). A heart rate of 120 to 130 beats per minute or less is an indicator of full recovery. Light activity such as jogging, walking, or shooting free throws should be performed during the rest period.

In order to bring about the training effect specific to the energy system, you must train at the proper intensity and allow sufficient time to replenish the system during the rest interval. Don't just jump into a high-intensity workout. Always remember to warm up and stretch at the beginning of your training session.

The following are typical off-season, pre-season, and in-season basketball training regimens that I have found to be quite effective with the players with whom I work. The off-season program is implemented following a 4-week post-season recovery phase.

Off-Season Training

Activity	Approximate duration
Warm-up—jog	5 minutes
Stretch	15 minutes
Speed development and/or power (plyometric) drills	15 minutes
Court conditioning drills—aerobic and some anaerobic	20-60 minutes
*Optional activity—run, cycle, tennis, swim, etc.	Varies
Cool-down—jog, skip rope, game of "horse," etc.	5 minutes
Resistance training (3-4 days per week)	20 to 60 minutes
Abdominal and low back strengthening	150 to 250 reps
Cool-down and stretch	10 minutes

Note: Many of the above activities are performed on alternate days. Some players like to lift during a second training session (e.g., "run" morning; "lift" afternoon). A typical off-season workout will last no longer than 2.5 hours per day.

Pre-Season Training

Activity	Approximate duration
Warm-up—jog, skip rope, stationary cycle, etc.	10 minutes
Stretch	10 minutes
Plyometrics—moderate to high intensity (2-3 days per week)	Varies
Speed development drills	20 minutes
Agility and coordination drills (alternate days to plyometrics)	Varies
Basketball skills (e.g., shooting, dribbling, etc.)	30-60 minutes
Court conditioning drills—anaerobic and technique	10-40 minutes
Functional strength—medicine ball, hills, harnesses, stairs, etc.	10-15 minutes
Cool-down—jog, skip rope, game of "horse," etc.	10 minutes
Resistance training (3-4 days per week)	20-60 minutes
Abdominal and low back strengthening	200-400 reps
Cool-down and stretch	10 minutes

Note: Not all of the above activities have to be performed each day. A pre-season session will never exceed 3 hours per day. Several combinations of the above routine could be achieved with dual sessions. Examples: (a) run in the morning and shoot and lift in the afternoon, or (b) shoot in the morning and run and lift in the afternoon.

Remember that all technique work such as shooting, speed development drills, plyometrics, agility drills, and so on, should be performed while you're fresh and therefore should precede all high stress activities such as resistance training, court conditioning drills, functional strength, and so on.

In-Season Training

Activity	Approximate duration
Warm-up—jog	3-5 minutes
Stretch—standing routine (all stretches while standing)	5-8 minutes
Second warm-up—**court conditioning drills**, speed drills, etc.	5 minutes
Second stretch—floor routine (all stretches, down on the floor)	5-8 minutes
Abdominal and low back strengthening	100-200 reps
Agility/coordination drills (plyometrics approx. 1 day per week)	Varies
Court conditioning drills—technique and some anaerobic	5-30 minutes*
Basketball practice	1-2 hours
Cool-down and stretch—free throws, jog, game of "horse," etc.	5-10 minutes
Resistance training	20-40 minutes
Cool-down and stretch	5-10 minutes

*Due to time constraints, in-season court conditioning drills are usually high-intensity, anaerobic activities with a 1:1 work-rest ratio (i.e., drill for 30 seconds, rest for 30 seconds). Often the conditioning drill period will last only 5 to 30 minutes, so you must get the most out of each minute.

During the season, games, travel schedules, and gym availability will constantly change when, where, and how long you can work out. Remember to perform all basketball skill development and high intensity technique work before any of your conditioning activities. Because the practice plans I've presented emphasize conditioning rather than technique work, the drills are placed in the middle of the workout. When practices emphasize skill development, court drills should follow all technique work.

Lifting during the season is mandatory for the Knicks. Frequency and duration drop but intensity remains high. Some players like to lift before practice; however, I recommend that resistance training be performed after practice.

CHAPTER 11

CONDITIONING WORKOUTS FOR EVERY SEASON

This chapter will present sample daily workouts that emphasize the use of the court conditioning drills presented in chapters 8 and 9. Use these examples as a general guide to help you design your own individual training routine. From these samples you'll find it simple to set up a program tailored to your needs.

Note that the duration of the workouts are close approximations, based on average times performed by several of the New York Knicks' players. Achieving the times is not as important as maintaining the appropriate work-rest ratio corresponding to the *purpose* of the training session (e.g., technique, anaerobic, or aerobic).

Four situations are presented: one player, three players, six players, and a full team (12 to 15 players). Examples for each of the preceding situations will be presented for the following seasonal phases: off-season, pre-season, and in-season. Since the focus here is on the development of the energy system specific to basketball, only the court drills are presented. Other practice activities such as warm-up, stretching, and resistance training have been intentionally omitted from the workouts that follow.

A special note to the coach: Be aware that factors such as the conditioning and ability levels of your players, game and travel schedules, school and personal commitments, and a host of other considerations will strongly influence the intensity, duration, and frequency of training.

Key to Workouts

I = **Individual (e.g., I-22 means Individual Drill #22)**
T = **Team (e.g., T-3 means Team Drill #3)**
C = **Continuous**

**Rotation free throws work best with 3 to 6 players per basket. Each player shoots 2 free throws then rotates clockwise. Other players are circled evenly around the free throw lane with one player directly under the basket to rebound for the shooter. Each time a new shooter rotates to the free throw line, a different player will have rotated to the rebounding position.

OFF-SEASON

1-Player Off-Season Workout

Emphasis and rest: Aerobic; minimal rest between sets

Duration: Approx. 29-35 min

Intensity: Low

Note: The duration for continuous reps/round trips is predetermined by the coach/player

Drill	Reps/ round trips	Sets	Duration (sec/set)	Rest interval
1. I-7	C	2*	30	No rest between sets 15 sec rest between drills 1 and 2
2. I-11	3	2	120-140	25 90°"ab" crunches after each set
3. I-8	C	2	120-180	5 free throws after each set
4. I-14	2**	2	160-190	25 low "ab" crunches after each set
5. I-4	5	1	140-150	30 sec rest between drills 5 and 6
6. I-4	5	1	140-150	30 sec rest between drills 6 and 7
7. I-22	1	1	75-85	5 free throws between drills 7 and 8
8. I-22***	1	1	75-85	25 90°"ab" crunches after each set
9. T-8	1	5	20-30	Walk/jog back to start (15 sec) and begin next set

  *One each way
  **End second rep/round trip with lay-up at position 17
***Use variation #1

OFF-SEASON

3-Player Off-Season Workout

Emphasis and rest: Aerobic; minimal rest between sets

Duration: Approx. 21-30 min

Intensity: Low

Note: The duration for continuous reps/round trips is predetermined by the coach/player

Drill	Reps/ round trips	Sets	Duration (sec/set)	Rest interval
1. T-3	C	1	120-180	15 sec rest between drills 1 and 2
2. T-13	C	3	30-90	15 sec rest after each set
3. I-12	1	3	40-50	15 sec rest after each set. Stagger start so players begin at 15-sec intervals
4. I-9	5	2*	160-190	25 90° "ab" crunches after each set. Stagger start; jog from position 5 back to 1; switch directions after 5 reps.
5. I-10	3	5	80-110	30 sec rest after each set. Stagger start, second player starts when first player reaches position 4 (use 2 or 3 balls). First player starts the next rep after third player completes the previous rep.

*One each way

OFF-SEASON

6-Player Off-Season Workout

Emphasis and rest: Aerobic; minimal rest between sets

Duration: Approx. 30-44 min

Intensity: Low

Note: The duration for continuous reps/round trips is predetermined by the coach/player

Drill	Reps/ round trips	Sets	Duration (sec/set)	Rest interval
1. I-3*	1	3	30-40	15 sec rest after each set. Players perform drill simultaneously evenly spaced on floor.
2. T-10	C	2	60-120	30 sec rest after each set. Stagger start; maintain even spacing.
3. T-11	C	2	60-120	30 sec rest after each set. Alternate starting position to work opposite direction. Remove all cones before beginning drill 4.
4. T-19	C	6	120-180	25 90° "ab" crunches after each set. Alternate direction (clockwise, then counterclockwise) between each set. Stagger start; maintain even spacing.
5. I-19	C	2	15-30	Each group performs "ab" crunches while other group runs drill. All athletes perform 25 low "ab" crunches between drills 5 and 6.
6. T-13	C	3	30-60	15 sec rest after each set
7. T-1	2	3	60-70	Slower running time = 15 sec rest after each set. Faster running time = 30 sec rest after each set.

*Eliminate rim/backboard taps

OFF-SEASON

Off-Season Team Workout

Emphasis and rest: Aerobic; minimal rest between sets

Duration: Approx. 25-36 min

Intensity: Low

Note: The duration for continuous reps/round trips is predetermined by the coach/player

Drill	Reps/ round trips	Sets	Duration (sec/set)	Rest interval
1. T-2	1*	2	75-90	25 low "ab" crunches after each set. No rest between drill options.**
2. T-1	3	3	90-105	Faster running times = 30 sec rest after each set. Slower running time = 15 sec rest after each set.**
3. T-4	C	1	120-180	30 sec rest between drills 3 and 4
4. T-8	1	8	20-30	Group 1 rests while Group 2 completes the set. No rest between drills 4 and 5.
5. T-14	C	1	60-180	30 sec rest between drills 5 and 6
6. T-5	C	1	60-180	No rest between reps/round trips. Immediately repeat in opposite direction. No rest between drills 6 and 7.**
7. T-3	C	2	120-180	50 90° "ab" crunches after each set

*One rep/round trip includes *all* eight drill options
**Players perform drill simultaneously, spaced evenly along baseline

PRE-SEASON

1-Player Pre-Season Workout

Emphasis and rest: Anaerobic; approx. 1:1 work-rest ratio

Duration: Approx. 29-40 min

Intensity: Moderate to high

Note: The duration for continuous reps/round trips is predetermined by the coach/player

Drill	Reps/ round trips	Sets	Duration (sec/set)	Rest interval
1. I-1	C	3*	15-45	15-45 sec of free throws or rest after each set
2. I-13	3	2	90-110	60 sec of 90° "ab" crunches and rest for remaining time after each set
3. I-14	2**	2	140-160	90 sec of free throws and rest for remaining time after each set
4. I-10	3	2	75-95	30 sec of "skywalkers" and rest for remaining time after each set
5. I-8	C	1	30-90	30 sec of low "ab" crunches and rest for remaining time after each set
6. I-17	3	2	100-115	60 sec of free throws and rest for remaining time after each set

*Set 1 normal; set 2 variation #1; set 3 variation #3
**End second rep/round trip with lay-up at position 17

PRE-SEASON

3-Player Pre-Season Workout

Emphasis and rest: Anaerobic; approx. 1:1 work-rest ratio

Duration: Approx. 25-35 min

Intensity: Moderate to high

Note: The duration for continuous reps/round trips is predetermined by the coach/player

Drill	Reps/ round trips	Sets	Duration (sec/set)	Rest interval
1. I-18	C	5	15-45	15-45 sec rest after each set
2. T-25	1	2*	120-130	Rest only during player rotation
3. I-23	3	2	75-110	Player 1 performs "ab" crunches until Player 2 completes set. Then Player 1 rests/rebounds during Player 3's set
4. T-22	C	2**	30	Rest only during player rotation

*One set of 3 reps/round trips per player each direction
**One 30 sec set per player on each side of basket

Note: Many times when players are working together, it becomes difficult to strictly adhere to a 1:1 work-rest ratio. Realize that resting players are actually active during their rest intervals (i.e., performing abdominal exercises, rebounding/passing to the working players, etc.).

PRE-SEASON

6-Player Pre-Season Workout

Emphasis and rest: Anaerobic; approx. 1:1 work-rest ratio

Duration: Approx. 13-19 min

Intensity: Moderate to high

Note: The duration for continuous reps/round trips is predetermined by the coach/player

Drill	Reps/ round trips	Sets	Duration (sec/set)	Rest interval
1. I-25	3	5	40-50	Group 1 rests while Group 2 completes the set. No rest between drills 1 and 2.
2. T-12	1*	5	20-25	Group 1 rests while Group 2 completes the set. No rest between drills 2 and 3.
3. T-7**	C	3***	30-60	Group 1 rests while Group 2 completes the set.

*All six cones equal one round trip

**Several "squares" are required to accommodate large numbers of athletes. Can be run with four athletes per "square."

***Three sets per player; 2-4 players per "square"

PRE-SEASON

Team Pre-Season Workout

Emphasis and rest: Anaerobic; approx. 1:1 work-rest ratio

Duration: Approx. 31-35 min

Intensity: Moderate to high

Note: The duration for continuous reps/round trips is predetermined by the coach/player

Drill	Reps/ round trips	Sets	Duration (sec/set)	Rest interval
1. T-3	C	1	120	30 sec rest; 60 sec of low "ab" crunches; rest for remaining time after drill 1
2. T-14	4	3	60-80	60-80 sec rest after each set
3. T-1	2	3	55-60	55-65 sec rest after each set
4. T-17	C	2	120	30 sec rest; 60 sec of 90° "ab" crunches; rest for remaining time after each set
5. T-20	C	2	120	30 sec rest after each set; 60 sec of "skywalkers"; rest for remaining time after each set

IN-SEASON

1-Player In-Season Workout

Emphases and rest: Technique and anaerobic
For drills lasting 1-60 sec, approx. 1:3 to 1:2 work-rest ratio
For drills lasting 60-180 sec, approx. 1:2 to 1:1 work-rest ratio

Duration: Approx. 19-26 min

Intensity: High—**all out!**

Note: The duration for continuous reps/round trips is predetermined by the coach/player

Drill	Reps/ round trips	Sets	Duration (sec/set)	Rest interval
1. I-2	C	3*	30	1:3 to 1:2 work-rest ratio; 60 sec of free throws after each set
2. I-15	1	2	50-60	1:2 work-rest ratio; 120 sec of free throws after each set
3. I-16	1	2	30-40	1:3 to 1:2 work-rest ratio; 80 sec of free throws after each set
4. I-11	2	2	65-80	1:2 work-rest ratio; 150 sec of free throws after each set

*Set 1 variation #1; set 2 variation #2; set 3 variation #3

IN-SEASON

3-Player In-Season Workout

Emphases and rest: Technique and anaerobic
For drills lasting 1-60 sec, approx. 1:3 to 1:2 work-rest ratio
For drills lasting 60-180 sec, approx. 1:2 to 1:1 work-rest ratio

Duration: Approx. 20-30 min

Intensity: High—all out!

Note: The duration for continuous reps/round trips is predetermined by the coach/player

Drill	Reps/ round trips	Sets	Duration (sec/set)	Rest interval
1. I-23	1	2*	25-35	1:3 work-rest ratio; 30 sec of 90° "ab" crunches; rest for remaining time after each set
2. T-15	C	3	30-60	1:2 work-rest ratio; 60-120 sec of rotation** free throws after each set
3. I-22	1	2	60-80	1:2 work-rest ratio. Rest for Player A is limited to total time for Players B and C to complete set (approx. 120-160 sec). Rotation: shooter to rebounder, rebounder to passer, passer to shooter.
4. I-11	2	2	65-80	1:2 work-rest ratio. Rest for Player A is limited to total time for Players B and C to complete set (approx. 130-160 sec). Rotation: shooter to spectator, spectator to rebounder/passer, rebounder/ passer to shooter.

*Two sets for each player (one round trip each way)
**See note on p. 234

![IN-SEASON banner]

IN-SEASON

6-Player In-Season Workout

Emphases and rest: Technique and anaerobic
For drills lasting 1-60 sec, approx. 1:3 to 1:2 work-rest ratio
For drills lasting 60-180 sec, approx. 1:2 to 1:1 work-rest ratio

Duration: Approx. 18-22 min

Intensity: High—all out!

Note: The duration for continuous reps/round trips is predetermined by the coach/player

Drill	Reps/ round trips	Sets	Duration (sec/set)	Rest interval
1. I-24	1	3	25-35	1:3 work-rest ratio. Note: Players work in pairs. After 1 set each for all 3 pairs has been completed, allow additional 30 sec rest. Switch partners and repeat until each player completes 3 sets total.
2. T-6	C	3	30	1:3 work-rest ratio. Note: Players work in pairs. All 3 pairs should perform this drill simultaneously evenly spaced on floor. After each set, rest 90 sec, switch partners and vary offensive and defensive position.
3. T-16	5*	3	25-30	Player rotation provides adequate recovery

*Start and finish will be at opposite ends of the line. So for this drill only down and back does not equal one rep/round trip. Instead, down the line once equals one rep/round trip. This drill requires five reps.

IN-SEASON

Team In-Season Workout

Emphases and rest: Technique and anaerobic
For drills lasting 1-60 sec, approx. 1:3 to 1:2 work-rest ratio
For drills lasting 60-180 sec, approx. 1:2 to 1:1 work-rest ratio

Duration: Approx. 20 min

Intensity: High—**all out!**

Note: The duration for continuous reps/round trips is predetermined
by the coach/player

Drill	Reps/ round trips	Sets	Duration (sec/set)	Rest interval
1. T-18	C	1	120	1:1 work-rest ratio; 120 sec of rotation** free throws after each set
2. T-23*	C	2	120	1:1 work-rest ratio; 120 sec of rotation** free throws after each set. Work opposite side of basket for the second set.
3. T-21	C	1	120	1:1 work-rest ratio; 120 sec of rotation** free throws after each set
4. T-20	C	1	120	After final drill, 30 sec rest; 30 sec of low "ab" crunches; 30 sec of 90° "ab" crunches; 30 sec of "skywalkers"

*This drill can be done using 2 baskets with 3 players working both
sides of the floor. Communication is important to avoid collisions. If
possible, it's best to have only 1 group of 3 players per basket.
**See note on p. 234

ABOUT THE AUTHOR

The author with his father, Dean Brittenham

Greg Brittenham is the strength and conditioning coach of the New York Knicks and has helped condition NBA basketball pros such as Patrick Ewing, Doc Rivers, and Derek Harper, as well as players from the Orlando Magic and Indiana Pacers. He is also president of Sport Elite Ltd., a leading organization that promotes athletic performance, human health, and physical fitness through education, research, training, and service.

Brittenham has been a leader in athletic conditioning since 1978, and was co-director for the Center for Athletic Development at the National Institute for Fitness and Sport in Indianapolis. He holds a master's degree in kinesiology from Indiana University and is a Certified Strength and Conditioning Specialist (CSCS). He is a member of the National Strength and Conditioning Coaches Association, the American College of Sports Medicine, and the National Basketball Conditioning Coaches Association.

An avid spokesperson for the importance of athletic conditioning, Brittenham has presented and demonstrated his training methods and programs to several prominent athletic groups, including the United States Tennis Association and the United States Olympic Committee (USOC).

Brittenham lives in Stamford, Connecticut with his wife, Luann, and their two children, Max and Rachel.